"Darius and I met over thirty-one years ago. I guess you could say he caught my heart back then, and he still has it today. Darius was in the Marine Corps when we first met on October 24th, 1992. He went overseas, and I didn't see him again until May of 1993. We did not waste any time and got married on September 18th, 1993. I can say Darius has always revered and deeply loved God. Through our marriage, Darius really discovered who I Am (Jesus) is to him by being a husband, a father to our three sons and two daughters in love (Darius & Danielle, Tyiler & Rixi, and Camren), a provider, a servant of the Lord, and in one of his newest roles of being Papu to our grandchildren. He has taught and modeled how godly men love and take care of their families. I am truly honored to be called Mrs. Darius C. Montgomery and to witness how the Lord is leading and guiding my husband through this journey of life. Darius has grown so much in these past years as he has allowed God to pour into him what needed to be poured while simultaneously healing the hurt and pain. Through writing these devotionals, I have seen how much God has favored him and has given him His godly wisdom. *Discovering Who I Am (In the 40)* is a devotional book for all ages. While you read it, allow the Holy Spirit to show you things that may need to be changed. My favorite devotional is *Your Greeting*—if we greeted one another in this way, no one would feel alone, and everyone would know they are blessed. This is exactly how we should greet one another. I am not going to spoil it, because you need to read it for yourself!"

—Loving you,
Your wife, Alecia A. Montgomery
Master's Art Teaching, Elementary School Teacher

"I have had the pleasure of knowing Darius and the Montgomery family for nearly thirty years. They are a rare example of perseverance, faithfulness, and maturity. This book, I believe, is a reflection of that dedication. Darius Montgomery has done a great job creating *Discovering Who I AM*. It is a great book on discipleship and truly learning how to follow Christ by using simple biblical truths. I love how he unpacks the forty days from a God-centered perspective. He incorporates amazing, life-changing experiences that were lived out during a forty-day pilgrimage with Christ. This devotional is a quick and powerful tool with thought-provoking teachings, and it allows the reader to consume each one with ease. It's like a well-prepared meal that is easily digestible and highly nutritional. I pray that you enjoy this forty-day journey and discover who you are in Christ as you grow in your faith so that you can walk in the benefits that the work of Jesus Christ offers you."

——Diego Mesa,
Founding Pastor
Abundant Living Family Church

DISCOVERING
WHO
I AM
[IN THE 40]

DARIUS C. MONTGOMERY

innovo
PUBLISHING

Published by Innovo Publishing, LLC
www.innovopublishing.com
1-888-546-2111

Innovo
PUBLISHING

Publishing Books, eBooks, Audiobooks, Music, Screenplays, & Courses for the Christian & wholesome markets since 2008.

DISCOVERING WHO I AM
(In the 40)

Library of Congress Control Number: 2024918243
ISBN: 978-1-61314-892-1

Cover Design & Interior Layout: Innovo Publishing, LLC

Printed in the United States of America
U.S. Printing History
First Edition: 2024

Has God called you to create a Christ-centered or wholesome book, eBook, audiobook, music album, screenplay, or online course? Visit Innovo's educational center (cpportal.com) to learn how to accomplish your calling with excellence.

CONTENTS

FOREWORD

I t is with great joy and deep respect that I share these words for my dear friend Darius' devotional book, *Discovering Who I Am*. Darius is an incredible husband and father and a devoted follower of Christ. Very few people over decades have shown their faithfulness to God as a disciple of Christ and pillar in the local church. His life is a testament to the transformative power of faith, and this book is a true reflection of his heart and his relationship with Jesus.

The title of this book is a profound play on words, highlighting God's declaration in Exodus 3:14, "I Am has sent me to you." This devotional invites readers to discover who God is within them, aligning their lives with His divine purpose. Each day is a fresh illumination of God's Word and how we can apply it in our lives.

Truly a Spirit-filled book with rich daily reflection, *Discovering Who I Am* is a spiritual roadmap designed to deepen our relationship with God. Each day, Darius presents scripture, reflections, and practical applications that encourage us to seek God wholeheartedly. This devotional is a reminder to daily "seek first the kingdom of heaven." As you delve into it, approach it with an open heart and a willingness to be transformed. Allow the words to guide you closer to God, to discover His presence, and to deepen your relationship with God.

—With heartfelt blessings,
Adam Mesa
Lead Pastor, Patria Church

ACKNOWLEDGMENTS & DEDICATION

I would like to dedicate this book to my Father, who allowed me, through the Holy Spirit, to write *Discovering Who I Am (in the 40)*. Without the Holy Spirit, there is no book.

I also want to acknowledge the following people. First, my wife, Alecia A. Montgomery, who has been with me throughout all of my shortcomings for over thirty years.

My sons, Darius Ross, Tyiler Cottrell, and Camren Alerius, who, in their own ways, showed me how God is always there and will never leave you. There were times I wanted to give up, but one of you boys would say something to keep me going.

My son Darius' wife, Danielle, and my son Tyiler's wife, Rixi: Since you two have come into my life, God has not only blessed me with daughters-in-law but with two *daughters* I always wanted in my life. Never forget you two are my daughters. One day, may He bless me with one more.

My grandchildren, Isabella, Brooklyn, and Shiloh: Papau loves you three and expects to share that love with your future first cousins.

My brother, Jacobi, who I am so proud of because many people will go through what you went through and throw in the towel. Keep that towel out of your hand and keep trusting in God.

My aunts Doris, Druscilla, and Elizabeth, and my uncles Leonard (no longer with us, but still in our hearts), Joseph, Leroy, and Amos. Each one of you shared in molding me into who I am. Thank you for being my sisters and brothers—closer than aunt and uncle relationships.

My pastor and friend, Pastor Diego: I say "thank you" because all the times we spent together really helped me to stay focused on the Lord. I know you will continue to allow the Holy Spirit to work through you.

My current pastor, Pastor Adam: I have seen you grow from a boy to a man of God. The anointing in you is so strong. Keep moving with the flow of the Holy Spirit.

My grandfather and grandmother raised me as their own. Thank you for pouring Christ into me, Mama. Daddy, I am grateful to God that He kept you until I got home in December 1995 to lead you to Christ.

My church family at Abundant Living Family Church and Patria. I truly appreciate the relationship I have with each and every one of you.

This book is dedicated to my former agent, Eurydice Davis. You were a beast of an agent who pushed me to be the best actor I could be.

My cousin Crystal L. Williams, who was like my little sister: There was a special day I remember when I was truly hurting, and you said, "Since you have been living for Christ, I have never seen you happier. You can't give that up. I will not let you." Thank you.

Finally, my mother, Audrey Mae Ham: I miss you and love you with all of my heart. Two things I truly thank God for—one, you were able to see some of my acting success, and two, you got to meet and love my wife and three sons.

This book is dedicated to anyone who is thinking about giving up and throwing in the towel. Tomorrow is another day, and your breakthrough is just a day away. Keep allowing God to wake you up so you can have a renewed spirit. And whatever you are going through, *this too shall pass.*

INTRODUCTION

S ome might say we cannot be "righteous" as sinful human beings. But you *can* be righteous by walking in the ways of the Lord. How do you achieve this? By accepting Jesus as your Savior and being born again in the Spirit, embracing faith, and dying to sin daily. See, Jesus, who never sinned, died to pay your sin debt—and God applies Christ's righteousness to you because you believe in Jesus through faith. Once you are born again in the Spirit, you have the power of the Holy Spirit to help you walk in "the ways of the Lord." You must seek the ways of God to be able to walk in the ways of God.

> *Blessed are those who keep His testimonies, Who seek Him with the whole heart! They also do no iniquity; They walk in His ways. (Psalm 119:2-3)*

> *But of Him you are in Christ Jesus, who became for us wisdom from God—and righteousness and sanctification and redemption. (1 Corinthians 1:30)*

> *He made Him who knew no sin to be sin on our behalf, so that we might become the righteousness of God in Him. (2 Corinthians 5:21)*

> *For if by the transgression of the one, death reigned through the one, much more those who receive the abundance of grace and of the gift of righteousness will reign in life through the One, Jesus Christ. (Romans 5:17 ESV)*

When you set out on a journey to discover something, it is always important to go to the source—or in this case, the

Source. *Discovering Who I Am* isn't just about discovering who you are but more so discovering who God is within you. When Moses asked who he should say sent him, God said, "I AM has sent me to you" (Exodus 3:14). The I AM, God, was simply stating to Moses that He exists and will always exist. "In the 40" in this book's title reflects on the forty days and forty nights it rained on the earth during Noah's time; the forty days and forty nights Moses spent on Mount Sinai, and the forty days and forty nights Jesus fasted in the wilderness. There is just something significant about the number "40," which signifies new life, new growth, and transformation. Over the next forty days and forty nights, work through *Discovering Who I Am* to connect with God the Father, God the Son (Jesus Christ), and God the Teacher (the Holy Spirit), and ask for God to bring you to your place of transformation.

1

YOUR *ROAD*

¹³ Now behold, two of them were traveling that same day to a village called Emmaus, which was seven miles from Jerusalem. . . . ¹⁵ So it was, while they conversed and reasoned, that Jesus Himself drew near and went with them. ¹⁶ But their eyes were restrained, so that they did not know Him. . . . ³⁰ Now it came to pass, as He sat at the table with them, that He took bread, blessed and broke it, and gave it to them. ³¹ Then their eyes were opened and they knew Him; and He vanished from their sight. ³² And they said to one another, "Did not our heart burn within us while He talked with us on the road, and while He opened the Scriptures to us?"
—Luke 24:13, 15-16, 30-32

Cleopas and another man were walking on the road to Emmaus. They were sad and hurt because, according to their words, "The things concerning Jesus of Nazareth . . . was a Prophet." They thought this even though, as you read in the scriptures, the two of them were present with the disciples when they found out about His resurrection. They had obviously spent time with Jesus, but Scripture doesn't say they were disciples. So they just hung around Jesus and His disciples. The question is, *Who are you on the road with?* Jesus said in John 10:27, "My sheep hear my voice, and I know them, and they follow me." These men were walking on the road with Jesus and did not know Him, even after being around Him.

Are you walking with Jesus and don't know it's Him? Or are you walking with the devil and think it's Jesus? Study the Scriptures; open your eyes to Jesus. The problem is, there are some people who think they are on the road with Jesus, but they are not. Cleopas and his "road dog" didn't recognize Jesus until He broke bread with them. Was it because they only thought of Jesus as a prophet? *If you are eating the right food (studying the Word on a daily basis), you will grow stronger in Christ. Just like a newborn getting the proper nutrition to grow strong in the body, you need the proper nutrition to grow strong in Christ.* By reading and studying scripture, you will discover the truth that Jesus was not merely a prophet—He was, is, and forever will be God. But I encourage you to read the Book (The Holy Bible). As you dive deeper into the Word of God, you will understand this clearly. (But you must study for yourself.)

The road you travel may be dusty and long, but when you are walking with Jesus, it's a road worth traveling. Yes, their eyes were open when Jesus broke bread with them, but their hearts were open because, as they said to each other, "He opened the Scriptures to us." *Sharing the Word with people will open their hearts to Jesus.* It will create a burning desire in their hearts. *Spending time fellowshipping with people will open their eyes to Christ. Who are you on the road with?* Or as a comedian used to say, "Who you wit!?"

Jesus, I thank You that You are on my journey with me. Show me how to share Your word with those who don't know You. Father, send the people to me whom You want on the road with me. Help me to be like Christ and share the scriptures to open their hearts to You, breaking bread with them to open their eyes to You through the Holy Spirit. In Jesus' name I pray. Amen.

2

YOUR *NAME*

23 "And in that day you will ask Me nothing. Most assuredly, I say to you whatever you ask the Father in My name He will give you. 24 Until now you have asked nothing in My name. Ask, and you will receive, that your joy may be full."
—*John 16:23-24*

The name of Jesus is powerful. The name of Jesus carries a lot of weight. There are some people's names you might mention, and people would automatically give you respect or anything you ask for. Take, for example, if you said to someone, "The president of the United States sent me here." People would automatically want to help you. No matter what or whose name you know, that name fails in comparison with the name of Jesus.

When Jesus was ready to enter Jerusalem, He asked two disciples to go and get Him a donkey and a colt. The thing is, the donkey and the colt belonged to someone, but Jesus told them, "If anyone says anything to you, you shall say, 'The Lord has need of them' and immediately he will send them." Just by mentioning the name of Jesus, the man let the disciples have what they were asking for. There is power in the name of Jesus. It's not just a phrase but the truth.

You may talk to someone about God today, and they might listen. The problem is, people are lost and think the universe, karma, a self-proclaiming person, or anything else is God. They are fooled, not realizing that their god is just a lowercase *god*. But once you mention the name *Jesus* to them, some people get combative. The name of Jesus causes things to stir or change in you on the inside. That's why there is no other name like Jesus. *Therefore, people get defensive when His name is mentioned because of the stirring they feel on the inside.* In Luke 10:17 we read, "Then the seventy returned with joy, saying, 'Lord, even the demons are subject to us in Your name.'" When was the last time you heard someone say that about anyone living or dead?

Jesus said, *"Whatever you ask the Father in My name He will give you." As soon as you say the name Jesus, you have an audience with God.* When you say that name above all other name, *Jesus*, all of heaven begins to listen. Sometimes things happen immediately, and sometimes things take time to change. One thing holds true: when you say the name *Jesus*, things *immediately begin* to change. Whose name are you calling on today?

Jesus, I love Your name because there isn't any other name that saved me. I will call on the name of Jesus all the days of my life. I will call on Your name, Jesus, in my tough times and especially in my good times. I stand here today and say that when things are good, it's only because of You, Jesus. I know that the name of Jesus is a strong tower, and I will stand firm on the name of Jesus. This is my pledge to You, heavenly Father. In Jesus' name I pray. Amen!

3

YOUR *FIRST*

17:1 You shall not sacrifice to the Lord your God a bull or sheep which has any blemish or defect, for that is an abomination to the Lord your God. 23:18 You shall not bring the wages of a harlot or the price of a dog to the house of the Lord your God for any vowed offering, for both of these are an abomination to the Lord your God.
—Deuteronomy 17:1; 23:18

What are you bringing to the Lord as your offering? The type of sacrifice in Deuteronomy 17:1 God doesn't ask for anymore. But He still requires a sacrifice. Your sacrifice may be your time, money, love, and even choice of career. Notice I said *your choice* of career, not God's choice for you. With your time, are you giving Him the best of your time or just the leftovers? With your money, are you giving the best or just what you have in your pocket at the time? *God wants you to always give your best to Him in all that you do.* Look at the time you are giving to Him. Are you saying, *God, I know I want to do this today, but I am going to spend time in prayer, worship, and studying your Word instead of watching the game or going shopping?* Or, *God, instead of taking my family on a vacation to Hawaii, I am going to take my family on a missions trip? Your time to God isn't just in prayer, worshipping, and studying but in serving and doing something that puts God first, no matter what you are going through in your life.*

There have been people over the years who have had wonderful and lucrative careers. Yet one day they heard from God and were told to give up their career for something greater. Think about the rich young ruler in Mark 10:17-22 who asked Jesus what he must do to inherit eternal life. When Jesus told him to sell all that he had and give it to the poor and to take up his cross and follow Him, he walked away with sadness and sorrow. He didn't want to make the sacrifice to follow Jesus. This is what God requires from you today: a sacrifice. Your sacrifice, be it your time, money, love, and even career. It's not just those things but whatever God is asking you today to sacrifice. As for your love, it can be as simple as what you love the most, whether that be games, a car, a cell phone, social media, money, people, or *whatever you put before God.*

Money is the big one for some people, especially when it seems like you don't have enough. God doesn't want your leftovers, your defects, or your sinful giving. Deuteronomy 23:18 above talks about the money that someone would use in a sinful way. God doesn't want any form of sin in the house of the Lord. He requires your best, always. Surely you know what a harlot is, but did you know "a dog" in this context refers to a male prostitute? God said, *Don't even bring me the money you were going to use to buy a male or female prostitute.* Why is that? Money is money, right? Wrong. It's because this person didn't put God first but thought to do something else with the money before giving it to God—and not just *anything* but something sinful. *No matter what, God wants to be put first in all things.* He always requires your best. Are you going to God in prayer first when you have a need or to someone else? *Give Him your first and your best and see how things change for you.* What are you bringing to the Lord as your offering?

> *Awesome and wonderful God, I will stop right now and give You my time of sacrifice. I don't want anything to be first in my life above or before You. I love You and will always give You my first—not my anything but my best of things. God, if I don't give You my best, I ask You to remind me of how I am falling short. I will always sacrifice to You my best offering. In Jesus' name I pray. Amen!*

_____

_____

_____

_____

_____

_____

_____

_____

_____

_____

_____

_____

4

YOUR *SEED*

"Is the seed still in the barn? As yet the vine, the fig tree, the pomegranate, and the olive tree have not yielded fruit. But from this day I will bless you."
—Haggai 2:19

G od used Haggai, the prophet, to talk to His people. God wanted them to understand that they put Him on the back burner. He told them in Haggai 1:7-9,

> *⁷Thus says the Lord of hosts: "Consider your ways! ⁸"Go up to the mountains and bring wood and build the temple, that I may take pleasure in it and be glorified," says the Lord. ⁹"You looked for much, but indeed it came to little; and when you brought it home, I blew it away. Why?" says the Lord of hosts. "Because of My house that is in ruins, while every one of you runs to his own house."*

Later He told them *after* they laid the foundation of the temple, "But from this day I will bless you." Once you put God first over all things in your life—even over your husband, wife, children, father, mother, friends, etc.— He puts you first because He wants to bless you. He wants to shower you with His love. He wants the best for you in your life. But for this to be, He must be first in your life.

My favorite part of this scripture is when Jesus said, *"Is the seed still in the barn?"* First, He reminds you that you still have seeds that can grow. *Yes, your seed is still in the barn. God is saying that once He is put first, He will water that seed because it needs to grow and not sit dormant.* Your seed, here, refers to your talents, gifts, abilities, and even just your love for God. *But you must make the choice to put God first.*

> *Today, my God, my God, I will not let my seed sit inside the barn. I will put You first in every part of my life. I will put You first above all things in my life. I welcome Your water that will flow in my life so I will never thirst again. Your living water will water my seeds and birth anew inside of me to grow for You. Thank You, Jesus, that Your blessings will rain down on my life, my family's life, my children's lives, my children's children's lives as I make the choice to put You first. In the mighty name of Jesus, the Son of God, I pray. AMEN!*

5

YOUR *LOVE*

¹⁰ One man of you shall chase a thousand, for the Lord your God is He who fights for you, as He promised you. ¹¹ Therefore take careful heed to yourselves, that you love the Lord your God.
—Joshua 23:10-11

Today, take pleasure in knowing that you are backed by the Word of God. You are covered by God's protection, and He is with you all the time. When you have someone in your life who is always there for you, it is easy to love them. God made a promise to be there for you through thick and thin. Not only that, but He said He will fight for you. *God made a promise that He will fight your battles.*

You can look at this in two ways. One: God will fight your battles. Two: He will fight for your love and attention. *Why would God fight for my love and attention*, you ask? *Isn't He God, so He doesn't need to fight for my love and attention?* That is true; He doesn't *need* to fight for it. Yet throughout your life, you will give love to other things and your attention will fall elsewhere. *God fights for your love and attention because He loves you!*

God doesn't fight for your love in the way you may think—like a spoiled child throwing a temper tantrum or like a baby crying for attention. God fights for your love and attention by being in the fight for you. God fights for your love and attention by correcting you when you are wrong. *God fights for your love and attention by showing you how much He loves you. When you are sick, He heals you. When you are hurting, He comforts you. When you are in need, He provides for you. When you are lost, He gives you direction. When you are falling into sinful ways, He is there to remind you of your need for holiness. When you don't feel loved, He surrounds you with His presence to show you how much you are loved by Him. This is how He fights for your love and attention. You are very special and precious to God, and that is why He fights for you. All God wants in return is your heart. He wants you to love Him. When you give God your heart and love, you will want to live for Him. You will want to live a life that is righteous and holy. He will always fight for you and love you; that is His promise.*

> *Heavenly Father and Loving God, I know that You love me. I am thankful that You fight for me. I am here to confess my love for You. I give You my heart today. Because of Your love for me, I ask You to correct me when I am falling into a sinful path. I want to live righteous and holy for You. I will keep You first in my life. I can never love You like You love me, but I will try to love You like You want me to love You. You are the one and only true God. I know You are God, Jesus, and the Holy Spirit. In Jesus' name I pray. Amen.*

_____

_____

_____

6

YOUR *REFUGE*

"The LORD repay your work, and a full reward be given you by the LORD God of Israel, under whose wings you have come for refuge."
—Ruth 2:12

You may be putting in godly work; you may be doing the things God asked of you; you may be staying faithful and standing on God's Word—but you don't see anything happening, and you don't see anything moving in your favor. Hear me: you don't see the wind, and yet do you see its effects? God will "repay your work."

James 2:20 says, "But do you want to know, O foolish man, *that faith without works is dead?"* Since, therefore, God requires you to have faith *and* works, you know that He will reward your works in Him. *For whatever you do unto the Lord, He will reward.* God sees your works, and He knows your needs. He will supply what is needed, and He will supply it fully. God doesn't ever, ever, ever do anything partially. The scripture says, God is *"a full reward."*

So *let the enemy attack you and keep pushing you* because, as the scripture says, *"under whose wings you have come for refuge."* All the enemy is doing is pushing you closer to God. Who, what, or where are you seeking refuge under? Seek your refuge under God. In the United States' Pledge of Allegiance it states, "One nation under God." All creation is under Him. It's important to know who you are under. *Let that be God.* Whom you position yourself under will *grow* you. Like a plant under the sun, soaking up what it needs to grow, you will receive what you need to grow from the Lord who is your covering. *Being under the Son will give you what you need to grow.* Who you position yourself under will *protect* you. Like using an umbrella for protection from the rain, *your faith in God and prayers to God are the umbrella* that will cover you. Who you position yourself under will *save* you. Like being in a hailstorm and going inside a house for safety, *God is your safe house. Where are you seeking refuge?*

> *The name of the LORD is a strong tower; The righteous run to it and are safe. (Proverbs 18:10)*

Heavenly Father, today I call on Your name, seeking refuge under You. I know that You see my works and will reward them. I will not do my works seeking Your reward but because I am doing the works You ask of me. I know I will receive Your full reward. I know You want me to live a blessed and prosperous life, not because of what I do but because of who You are. I come to You for refuge, and I know I am safe from everything that has, is, or will come against me. In Jesus' name I pray. Amen.

7

YOUR *COMBINATION*

Now when they began to sing and to praise, the Lord set ambushes against the people of Ammon, Moab, and Mount Seir, who had come against Judah; and they were defeated.
—2 *Chronicles 20:22*

I pray and I study the Holy Bible. But do I sing praises to Him? All of these things are like a combination lock. You may turn it to the first two digits to unlock the lock, but without that third digit, it won't unlock. As Christians who love the Lord, you must pray, study the Word, and sing praises to God. By all means this is not to say this is the only way to get things to move in your life. Like a combination lock, understand this: some things don't get unlocked without that third digit.

If you read the entirety of 2 Chronicles 20, you will see that the tribe of Judah was invaded. They prayed to God, and then they heard a word from God through Jahaziel: "Then the Spirit of the Lord came upon Jahaziel" (2 Chronicles 20:14a). But it wasn't until verse 22 when those who were appointed sang that God moved on the tribe of Judah's behalf. *You have access to (the combination for) God's heart, God's mercy, God's grace, God's blessing, and God Himself. Are you working on the combination today?*

It's time to unlock all that God has set aside for you. Take the time today to pray, study the Holy Bible, and sing praises. Remember, God doesn't require these things for His own glory but for you to live a complete life in Him. Psalm 134:1-2 says, "[1]Behold, bless the Lord, All you servants of the Lord, Who by night stand in the house of the Lord! [2] Lift up your hands in the sanctuary, And bless the Lord."

When you focus on God, He focuses on you. Have you noticed when you are busy that you can't focus, or you don't notice the other things that are happening around you? Imagine if you gave God all your attention. Imagine spending your time in prayer. *Imagine spending your time in His Word. Imagine spending your time singing praise and worship. Now, imagine what your life would look like if you did this daily.*

> *Oh Lord, I will spend time praying, singing, and reading Your Word. I will sing praise and worship to You daily. I will give You my full attention. Show me how to live my life with Your combination. I am Yours, and You are mine. I lift my hands to You totally in admiration. In Jesus' name I pray. Amen.*

_____

_____

_____

_____

_____

_____

8

YOUR *VOICE*

¹¹ Then He said, "Go out, and stand on the mountain before the Lord." And behold, the Lord passed by, and a great and strong wind tore into the mountains and broke the rocks in pieces before the Lord, but the Lord was not in the wind; and after the wind an earthquake, but the Lord was not in the earthquake; ¹² and after the earthquake a fire, but the Lord was not in the fire; and after the fire a still small voice.
—1 Kings 19:11-12

God is incredible and immeasurable, but sometimes when you are looking for God, you miss the small things He does for you. Elijah the prophet proved to the servants of Baal, Jezebel, and Israel that God is real through a display of His greatness. He later heard that Jezebel sought to kill him, so he became afraid and ran away into the wilderness. Elijah saw the greatness of God and was used by God to perform great things, but he ran away when trouble was coming. Elijah heard Jezebel sought to kill him, and he got afraid and ran. Are you like Elijah?

Elijah prayed for no rain due to the disobedience of God's people, and it didn't rain for three years. The rain only returned after Elijah prayed for it again. Elijah prayed for the widow's son to be revived after he fell sick and died, and the Lord brought him back to life! Elijah stood before King Ahab and four hundred fifty prophets of Baal and was not afraid of death as he spoke boldly about God. *First Kings 18:21 says, "And Elijah came to all the people, and said, 'How long will you falter between two opinions? If the Lord is God, follow Him; but if Baal, follow him.'"* Elijah was used by God to show how great God is. Why then did Elijah run away from Jezebel? He, before meeting with King Ahab, knew about Jezebel massacring the prophets of the Lord. *Elijah* means "the Lord is God." Yet, "elijah" still fled when Jezebel sent him a threatening letter. This elijah got scared of Jezebel's words and the situation that was coming. *This elijah*, for a moment, lost trust in his God.

Are you *elijah* (the one who runs from other people's negative words and threats) or are you Elijah (whose name means "the Lord is God")? You will have your *elijah* moments in your life, but you need to return to the Elijah moments by continually trusting God. When it all was said and done, *elijah* was looking for God in the great and mighty things—the strong wind, the earthquake, and the fire. But Elijah found God again in the still, small voice. He found God in a very gentle whisper. Why? Because God wanted *elijah* to stop running and to trust Him. When something is loud, it's easy for you to hear it. But when it's a gentle whisper, you have to be still and get closer to hear. God came to *elijah* in a gentle whisper to bring him close to Him. *He wanted elijah close to Him to remind Elijah who he was created to be—and that is Elijah. God has created you to be You not you.* When things get rough, listen for that still, small Voice, and you will not get lost. The still, small Voice is there to build you up and guide you to who God made you to be. You are great and greatly made. God doesn't want you to run from the things that come against you. He wants you to trust Him that He will bring you through whatever it is, no matter what it looks like. *He brings you through everything that you are going through! Remember He created you to be You! Just trust God.*

> *Great and mighty God, You are so immeasurable. How can I ever doubt that You have everything under control? How can I ever doubt that You know what will happen before it even is manifested? How can I doubt the You in me? How can I doubt You? I will trust the Lord with all my heart and all that is within me. I bless Your Holy Name. I will never doubt You anymore. I believe You will do what You said You will do. I will listen to Your still, small Voice. I will be drawn to You because of Your still, small Voice. I listen to You! I will do what You ask of me! I will trust You! I love You, Lord! In Jesus' name I pray. Amen!*

9

YOUR *SHOUT*

So, the people shouted when the priests blew the trumpets. And it happened when the people heard the sound of the trumpet, and the people shouted with a great shout, that the wall fell down flat. Then the people went up into the city, every man straight before him, and they took the city.
—Joshua 6:20

When you are going through something that seems impossible, you may wait until you get through it to shout. You may say to God, *Lord, if You get me through this, I will shout Your name on high.* This is backward thinking, not forward thinking. You need to believe that God can and will do anything for you according to His will. The Israelites were instructed to march around the walls of Jericho, remaining quiet for six days. The only people allowed to make a sound were the seven priests with ram horns, blowing continually as they marched around the wall once each day. There are two things about this story that you need to understand. First, you may think, after praying for your situation or after you had someone pray over your situation, that God is silent because He isn't moving. Second, you may think that you have to wait until after you are out of your situation before you can shout to God. The truth is, God is silent *because* He is moving on your behalf. Why are you waiting to give God the glory with a shout?

Shout your way through your situation. Don't sit silent as the enemy presses against you. March around your situation, praying, because your prayers are the priests' ram horns. This you should do continuously. After you have prayed over your situation, you need to shout to God and give Him the praise, believing with no doubt that your situational walls are falling down flat. The scripture doesn't say the walls came down and then the Israelites shouted to God. The scripture clearly says, "And it happened *when . . . the people shouted . . . that* the wall fell down flat." Your shouts of praise and thankfulness before your walls fall are the obedience you are called to as you wait.

This is where your faith is required. Some may say, "I have prayed, and I have shouted, giving God the praise, but my walls haven't fallen. What am I doing wrong?" What you need to do now is wait patiently on God. How long, you may ask? Until He answers your prayer. The problem is that some people don't know how to wait on the Lord. This is how you should wait on the Lord: *with no doubt, with no complaining, and with continuous prayer and shouting.* Joshua 6:16 says, "And the seventh time it happened, when the priests blew the trumpets, that Joshua said to the people: 'Shout, for the Lord has given you the city!'" *Did it happen on the first day? You have to pray and shout continuously over your situations. Why are you sitting in silence, allowing the enemy to beat you up? Open your mouth and shout to God because you know what you have prayed for is already complete. Is there anything too hard for God? It's time to stop sitting in silence, get up, and march around your situation with your ram horn of "prayer!" It's time to shout because you know you are victorious.*

God, I lift Your name up on high. I speak right now to [state the situations that you know someone else is going through]. I pray that those situations have fallen down in their lives, and they now have victory, in the name of Jesus. I thank You and praise You, God, because I know I am victorious over [state all of your situations]. I know, God, that nothing is too hard for You. The walls in my life will fall flat, in the name of Jesus. Every situation that is coming against me is now torn down. I know You have given me authority to speak to my situations and remove it from out my way through prayer. Because it's not by my strength that things change but by Your Power. In the name of Jesus, I pray. Amen!

10

YOUR *SILENCE*

And the man, wondering at her, remained silent so as to know
whether the Lord had made his journey prosperous or not.
—*Genesis 24:21*

S ilence is an amazing thing but also something that's
hard to do. In today's society, everyone likes to voice
their opinions, even to God. People will talk and talk to
God . . . continually. When was the last time you spoke
to God and "remained silent" to hear from Him? How
can you hear Him if you keep talking? The context of
this scripture is when Abraham's servant was tasked to
find a wife for Isaac. Once the servant got to the well,
he prayed, "O Lord God of my master Abraham, please
give me success this day, and show kindness to my master
Abraham" (Genesis 24:12). He finished his prayer by
saying, "And by this I will know that You have shown
kindness to my master" (Genesis 24:14).

Once the servant prayed, Rebekah made her way to
him at the well. The servant did exactly what he said he
would do in his prayer: "Now let it be that the young
woman to whom I say, 'Please let down your pitcher that
I may drink.'" He made this request of Rebekah, and she
responded favorably. The main point here is that once

the servant encountered Rebekah, he closed his mouth in order to hear from God. As this applies to your life today, you need to see the importance in being silent before God. At some point or another, you will ask God to do something in your life. If something or someone comes into your life that/who looks like what you prayed for, you may immediately start rejoicing instead of listening to see if what you've encountered truly is what God has prepared for you. Then, if things later go awry, you blame God. *Don't forget: the devil can hear you too (unless you are praying in the heavenly language through the Holy Spirit— tongues).* In Genesis 24 the servant closed his mouth and listened to God to make sure Rebekah was the answer to his prayer.

Genesis 24:26 says, "Then the man bowed down his head and worshiped the Lord." After the servant saw that this woman truly was the answer to his prayers, he bowed down and worshiped the Lord. You spend your time in prayer, worshiping God and studying His Word. *But through it all, are you listening to God? Are you remaining silent to hear what God has to say? Are you doing what Abraham's servant did and waiting for God to manifest your prayers? It's very important to pray, but it is even more important to listen.* Remember, a conversation with God is just that—a conversation. In order to have a conversation, one person talks while the other listens. But sometimes in your life, God does all the listening while you do all the talking. *It's time to make your conversation with God a conversation with God. After you pray, spend some time listening for the Voice of the Lord and where He is leading you. He will not lead you astray. Stop talking; now sit and listen.*

My God, I come to You now and ask You to speak to me. I want to hear from You, Lord. I want You to show me what I need to do in my situation. I trust that You will show me what I need to do. I will pray and keep silent so I can hear from You. Speak to me, Lord, clearly so I can follow where You are leading me. In Jesus' name I pray. Amen.

11

YOUR *IDENTITY*

*Then Haggai, the Lord's messenger, spoke the Lord's message to
the people, saying, "I am with you, says the Lord."*
—*Haggai 1:13*

Whom you hang around says a lot about you! People
sometimes associate you with the company you
keep. Are you careful about who you are with? Are you
careful about who's with *you*? In South Carolina, there
is a law that states, "the hand of one is the hand of all."
This means if someone commits a crime, anyone who is
with that person is charged with the same crime. It doesn't
matter if you participated. Just being with the person who
committed the crime will get you in trouble.

Now, isn't it wonderful that God said, "I am with you"?
God is with you; therefore He should be the one people
associate you with. But the question is, *Do you want to
just be associated with God, or do you want to be identified
with God? Today, it doesn't matter who you've hung around.
It doesn't matter what you have done. It doesn't matter who or
what you have associated with. It's time to find **your identity
in Christ.***

Since God is with you, it's time to say, *"I am with God!"* Claim your identity in Christ. God doesn't just associate Himself with you. He clearly said in scripture, *"with you."* *He will have your back. He will never leave you. He will stand for you! He is a part of you. He is connected to you. God wants you to know that you may be in the dark, but that light you see is God. That voice you hear is God. That peaceful presence you feel is God. He is with you, always!*

Matthew 10:22 says, "And you will be hated by all for My name's sake. But he who endures to the end will be saved." Don't be afraid of people identifying you with Christ. Carry your identification around you like dog tags or a badge. *Wear God's identity proudly and rejoice that the world hates you because of His Identity that's in you.* Continue to show God's love daily, and He will carry you through to the end.

Who do you want to be identified with?

> *Lord, I am proud to tell people You are with me, and I am with You! I want the world to identify me with You. I want the world to know I am walking with You. Regardless of how the world treats me, I will still love them. I will endure until the end. In Jesus' name I pray. Amen.*

12

YOUR *REPUTATION*

*11 But Jehoshaphat said, "Is there no prophet of the Lord here,
that we may inquire of the Lord here, that we may inquire of
the Lord by him?" So, one of the servants of the king of Israel
answered and said, "Elisha the son of Shaphat is here, who
poured water on the hands of Elijah." 12 And Jehoshaphat said,
"The word of the Lord is with him." So, the king of Israel and
Jehoshaphat and the king of Edom went down to him.*
—*2 Kings 3:11-12*

E lisha was not just any prophet. The anointing that was
upon him was double that of Elijah. See, Elijah told
Elisha that "if you see me when I am taken from you, it
shall be so for you." So it was as Elijah had spoken, and
this anointing was only known by Elijah, Elisha, and God.
Whether you have God in your life or not, your reputation
will precede itself. But as a Christian, you should desire the
Spirit of Christ to shine in you so your good reputation will
precede you.

Jehoshaphat the servant asked the question, "Is there no
prophet of the Lord?" He didn't know Elisha, but at the
mention of Elisha's name, Jehoshaphat immediately said,
"The word of the Lord is with him." This is how God works
with your name and reputation. People who don't know

you will know your name because of the God who lives in your heart—not because of anything you have done. There are many selfish "prophets" who only serve themselves, but God will use those who walk in humility to stand before those in authority as His representatives. Note what Jehoshaphat heard: "Elisha the son of Shaphat is here, *who poured water on the hands of Elijah.*" Jehoshaphat observed that Elisha was a servant. When you have a servant's heart, God will use you in front of kings. *Jehoshaphat knew that God was with Elisha because of who Elisha hung around—Elijah!*

Just like Elisha, your reputation is also established by whom you hang around with. The people whom you allow in your inner circle contribute to how others see you. This is why God continually told the Israelites to separate themselves from the people who were ungodly and *why God tells us not to be "unequally yoked together with unbelievers" (2 Corinthians 6:14).* This scripture as it relates to marriage also applies to other relationships—be it friends, family, co-workers, or any other type. The reason for this command is because it would be too easy to stumble and compromise your reputation. It's important to acknowledge that God does want you to associate with unbelievers and be a light in their darkness. *Romans 14:16 (KJV) says, "Let not then your good be evil spoken of." Jesus hung out with unbelievers and did not indulge in their sinful ways. So, then, let your godliness precede you so that God will present you before kings who will know your name.*

Heavenly Father, I thank You for being my God and the Creator of all. I thank You that the reputation You have established in me will precede me. I thank You that Your godliness in me will shine so bright that no matter what the devil tries to say about me, Your light will prevail. I will always follow You so that others will not see who I am but the I AM, Jesus Christ. I will be Your humble servant so that when I stand before unbelievers, they will already know who I am because of the Jesus Who's inside of me. I thank You that You will use my reputation to open doors for me to speak to unbelievers. In Jesus' name I pray. Amen!

13

YOUR *HOLINESS*

> *¹ And the Lord spoke to Moses saying, ² "Speak to all the congregation of the children of Israel, and say to them: You shall be holy, for I the Lord your God am holy."*
> —*Leviticus 19:1-2*

God wants you to live a holy life. What does this mean? In Leviticus 19, God gives a long list of things to do and not to do. But, after each one, He said, *"I am the Lord."* It's important to see God's omnipotence as you seek to live a holy life.

You may think that living holy as Jesus said—"for I the Lord your God am holy"—is too hard. But let's face it, it is easy for God to be holy because He has always been holy. Genesis 1:26 says, "Then God said, 'Let Us make man in Our image, according to Our likeness.'" You were created to be holy, just as God is holy. You were created in His image! But you must choose holiness. This is where some people have a problem. When you allow—yes, *allow*—sin to draw you away from God, you are not living holy. Living in holiness is drawing near to God and fleeing from sin.

God requires your holiness for a good and blessed life, and when you embrace this holiness, you will walk in your purpose. Every part of a tree serves a purpose, but if one part of the tree decides it doesn't want to be like the rest of the tree, then the tree will die. This world is dying as people who are part of God's tree make the conscious choice not to live holy in their purpose.

People are searching for something bigger than themselves, putting all their energy into things that are not of God— things that are unholy and sinful. Take a closer look at the last part of the scripture mentioned earlier and understand how to live holy: *"I the Lord your God am holy."* All you need to live holy is to know God and draw near to Him. You don't need anything in this world. *All you need is God!* Here is the thing that the people who seek after something else do not understand: *when you have God, you have everything.* God created and has dominion over everything, so *when you have Him, you have everything.*

Living in sin has one purpose, and that purpose is death. Living in God has many purposes, but the one you should focus on today is His holiness. Living holy is to be like your Father.

My Lord and Savior, I will live wholly because You are Holy. I know I was created in Your image, which makes it easier for me to live holy. I will to be like my Father. I will love like my Father. I will talk like my Father. I will share like my Father. I will talk to people like my Father. I will live like my Father. Now I know, Father, that to live holy is to live wholly. All I have to do is be like You. I must strive to be holy like my Father. In Jesus' name I pray. Amen.

14

YOUR *KNOWLEDGE*

My people are destroyed for lack of knowledge. Because you have rejected knowledge, I also will reject you from being priest for Me; Because you have forgotten the law of your God, I also will forget your children.
—Hosea 4:6

God wants you to understand who He is. It is important to *read* God's words in order to *study* God's words. If you just casually read a sign in passing, you may not understand what it says. But if you read the sign with intent to understand its meaning, you will find it. What if a sign said, *Danger?* Would you understand the meaning if you didn't know what the word meant? This is why God said, "My people are destroyed for lack of knowledge." In order to know God, you must have knowledge of God. Therefore, God blessed us with His anointed words through the writing of the Holy Bible.

In the beginning of Hosea 4, Hosea said to the Israelites, "Hear the word of the Lord." To grow in the wisdom and knowledge of God, you must study and hear the Word. Before parchment (a form of paper) was created, the only way to pass the Word of God was through speech. People would memorize all the information and then pass it on to the next generation. Genesis 1:3, 6, 9, 11, 14, 20, 24, and 26 include, *"Then God said."* Since God spoke everything into existence, He wants you to study and speak His Word as well—the *Holy Bible*.

Why was God warning the Israelites in Hosea 4:1b: "There is no truth or mercy or knowledge of God in the land"? Because they drifted so far away from Him that they started embracing sin instead of turning away from it. *Knowledge of God leads you to the truth of God—the truth being Jesus. The truth of God allows you to receive the mercy of God—the mercy being Jesus. Receiving God's mercy leads you away from sin.*

In an 1817 letter to George Ticknor, Thomas Jefferson wrote, "The important truths [are] that knowledge is power, that knowledge is safety, and that knowledge is happiness." Studying God's words will guide you toward understanding the *"important truth." God is your safety; Jesus is your happiness; the Holy Spirit is your power. Since all three (God, Jesus, and the Holy Spirit) are one and the same, God is your safety, happiness, and power.* The phrase *"knowledge is power"* holds so true with God. With the knowledge of God, you have power! When you seek the perfect knowledge of God, you will see the truth. *God is your El Deah ("the God of knowledge").*

Father, El Deah, I thank You for giving me the knowledge of You. I receive You, God, as truth. I will study Your Word, the Holy Bible, to continually grow in my understanding of You, receiving new revelations every time I study Your Word through the Holy Spirit. I will speak Your Word over my life. I know You know all, and Your knowledge has no end. In Jesus' name I pray. Amen.

15

YOUR *BELIEF*

For God so loved the world that He gave His only begotten Son, that whoever believes in Him should not perish but have everlasting life.
—John 3:16

When was the last time you gave something away and didn't ask for anything in return? You may have given some loose change to someone on the street, not asking for anything in return. You may have given someone a birthday gift, not asking for anything in return. But truth be told, you do expect something from them—some form of *thank you.*

You may think that God's gift to you in His Son, Jesus, was not without assumption of response and gratitude. That what He wanted from you was to *believe in Him.* But God doesn't *ask* that you believe in Jesus; He *tells* you what you will gain if you believe in Christ. *This gift of Jesus comes not only with eternal life but with access to all of whom God is.* Yet some will reject this gift and perish because of lack of knowledge and an unwillingness to believe. Just because God gave the gift doesn't mean everyone will accept it.

People believe in wealth, power, drugs, sex, total control, or self-existence, and they *live* for these things. But God is greater than all things in existence! *Who or what you live for will either condemn you or sanctify you.* John 3:18 says, "He who believes in Him is not condemned; but he who does not believe is condemned already, because he has not believed in the name of the only begotten Son of God." *What you believe in will define who you are.*

What are you believing in today? Some people believe God sends the unrepentant to hell. John 3:17 says, *"For God did not send His Son into the world to condemn the world, but that the world through Him might be saved."* Therefore, no, God does not *send* unbelievers to hell. They have simply rejected His free gift and chosen the path to destruction. Others ask, "Why do I have to believe in Jesus Christ?" Within this question lies the conundrum of free will. Everyone loves it, but no one knows its depth. *Your belief will cause your eternal demise! There is one thing people love but don't truly understand or even appreciate—free will.* God said, "*whoever believes in Him*"—Him being Jesus Christ. *You must believe with all your heart! And this choice to believe is yours to make.* Have you made the choice? *God's love for you is the reason He gave you Jesus.* Accept God's gift of true love, then pass it on so someone else can make the choice.

> *Awesome and amazing Father, I believe in You. I believe in Christ the Son. I believe in the Holy Spirit. I believe in the resurrection. I believe in the name of Jesus Christ. I believe in You. I thank You, Father, for believing in me, Your precious creation. In the name of Jesus I pray because I believe. Amen!*

16

YOUR *CALL*

¹⁹ God is not a man, that He should lie, Nor a son of man, that He should repent. Has He said, and will He not do? Or has He spoken, and will He not make it good? ²⁰ Behold, I have received a command to bless; He has blessed, and I cannot reverse it.
—Numbers 23:19-20

Has someone ever said they would do something but later changed their mind and decided not to do it? Often, we find our fulfillment in our personal relationships. But unfortunately, people will always let us down. God will never change His mind on you. He said that once He blesses you, no one can change that. Isn't that remarkable? That God will always tell you the truth, no matter what? And that once He says He will do something, it is done. *The truth is your blessing was completed the moment God spoke it into being—not the moment you received it.* God's words allow goodness in your life. Are you allowing God to speak to you? Have you received the promises God has made to you? Wait patiently on His promise to you. It is coming, because *"God is not a man, that He should lie."*

"Behold, I have received a command to bless." God puts people in your path to be blessings for you. However, because we are fallen creatures, these people may not always do what the Lord asks of them. Does that mean you will not receive your blessing? No, far from it! What it means is that *God will line up someone else to bless you*—even where you least expect it. See, when someone doesn't answer *God's call to bless*, they aren't hurting your blessing but their own. Think about 1 Kings 17:8-16. Elijah was told by God to go and live with a widow. The widow didn't have anything but a little flour and oil to make a small morsel of bread for her and her son. After that was gone, they wouldn't have any more food. But God told the widow to bless Elijah, and she answered His call. Once she blessed Elijah even though she knew she didn't have enough, her flour and oil didn't run out until it rained—which came also to bless her. By Elijah answering the call, the widow woman and her son were blessed. *But she had to answer God's call to receive her own blessing.*

When you answer God's call to bless someone, you also receive a manifold blessing. And God will sustain you until you receive your blessing. Are you going to say yes to God? Who is God asking you to bless today?

> *God, I am so thankful that You are not a man, that You should lie. I thank You, Father, for the people You have put in my path to be a blessing to me. But I rejoice, Lord, because of the people You have put in my path for me to bless. I will answer Your call to bless. In Jesus' name I pray. Amen.*

17

YOUR *WAYS*

When a man's ways please the Lord, He makes even his enemies to be at peace with him.
—Proverbs 16:7

S ometimes it looks like things aren't working out for you. You put in all the effort, and yet everything still seems to come against you. But God said that if you would seek to please Him with all your ways, He would cause your enemies to have peace with you.

While you walk in the ways of the Lord, God works in the situations that surround you. *Persist in the ways of God, and you will see the things you seek.* He wants you to follow Him not for His benefit but for <u>yours</u>. As a parent rejoicing in their child's achievements, so God is pleased when you accomplish tasks unto the Lord. God will celebrate with you and prepare your path forward.

Let God celebrate you today in pleasing Him by the way you carry yourself. If something doesn't go as planned, don't worry; continue to pursue Him, and watch how your situation changes. God's will *will* be done despite any circumstances in your lives. You may get hurt, or you may not want to follow where God is leading you, but God will always give you what is best for you. *So, when you choose to follow His lead, the Lord will bless you.*

David, when he was running from King Saul, took refuge with the Philistines. They knew who he was, but because David ways pleased God, they did not kill him. They actually welcomed him! If God can do that for David, what will He do for you? If you want things to change and move for you, *"Seek ye first the kingdom of God"* (Matthew 6:33 KJV).

> *Dear God, I want my ways to please You. When people look at me, I want them to see You. Your ways will be my ways. I know when I have a heart after You, no matter what, things will always work out for my good. I thank You, knowing when my ways please You, even my enemies will be at peace with me. In Jesus' name I pray. Amen!*

18

YOUR *PLAN*

For I know the thoughts that I think toward you, saith the Lord,
thoughts of peace, and not of evil, to give you an expected end.
—Jeremiah 29:11 (KJV)

The New International Version (NIV) says, "'For I know the plans I have for you,' declares the Lord, 'plans to prosper you and not to harm you, plans to give you hope and a future.'" Do you know the plan God has for your life? Do you believe in His plan? Do you trust His plan? God had a plan for your life before you were even born. God spoke in Jeremiah 1:5: "Before I formed you in the womb, I knew you; Before you were born, I sanctified you." He spoke to John the Baptist's father, Zacharias, in Luke 1:15: "For he will be great in the sight of the Lord and shall drink neither wine nor strong drink. He will also be filled with the Holy Spirit, even from his mother's womb." Are you an exception to what God said in those two verses? *No, because God never changes.* If God knew Jeremiah and John the Baptist before they were in the womb and set their plan in motion before they were born, He has done the same for you. But like Jeremiah and John, *you must embrace God's plan for your life and accept your calling.*

It can be tough to accept God's plans for your life. You may think this means giving your life over to God so that He can control it. This is far from the truth. The parents of the lion will teach him how to be what he was created to be. Once the cub grows up, his parents will let him go and apply what he has been taught. When trouble comes, the cub's instruction will kick in like muscle memory. He will make mistakes, and he will learn from them. Just like the lion's parents don't want to control him, God doesn't want to control you. He wants you to know and trust the plan He has for you.

When you sync with God by accepting Jesus and receiving the Holy Spirit, you can discern the path in front of you. When you try to control the outcome, you will fail. *But when you trust God and let Him determine the outcome, you will never fail.* This path toward the outcome is often what people have issues with. If someone were to tell you that within ten years you will have everything, but you must first go to prison and get beaten and abused before you receive it, would you follow that path? Many would say "no," but the few that say "yes" will receive their reward. *Trust God today; He knows what He is doing,* and He has a special plan for each of you. *It's time to ask God what His plan is for your life. It's time to believe in His plan. It's time to trust in His plan.*

> *The one and only true God, I ask You to reveal Your plans for my life. I will believe the plans You have for me. I will trust Your plans for me. I believe and trust that the plans for my life were put into motion before I was even conceived. I will never doubt Your plans for me. I have purpose, and I thank You for instilling my purpose within me. I love You, Father. In Jesus' name I pray. Amen.*

19

YOUR *CHARACTER*

18:33 Then the king was deeply moved, and went up to the chamber over the gate, and wept. And as he went, he said thus: "O my son Absalom—my son, my son Absalom—if only I had died in your place! O Absalom my son, my son!" 19:1 And Joab was told, "Behold, the king is weeping and mourning for Absalom."
—*2 Samuel 18:33–19:1*

This scripture deals with how to be a person of character. David truly was a person of character. Therefore, God said, "David had a heart after Him." Even at his worst, David showed true character. When he committed adultery with Bathsheba and then had her husband, Uriah, killed to hide his sin, he owned up to his actions when confronted by the prophet Nathan. David didn't say, "Well, if Bathsheba wasn't out on the rooftop bathing, this wouldn't have happened." He didn't try to hide it or put blame on someone else.

Now look at 2 Samuel 18:33–19:1. Absalom killed his brother Amnon because he violated their sister Tamar. But David forgave Absalom, just like he had forgiven Amnon. Then Absalom stole the throne from his father. Yes, David should have punished Amnon for his sinful act. But look at David's heart and mindset: he forgave his son Amnon. Every time David fell short of God's glory, God forgave him. David recognized that no one is perfect, and since God forgave him, he should forgive others. This was the character of David. Proverbs 24:17-18 says, *"Do not rejoice when your enemy falls, and do not let your heart be glad when he stumbles; Lest the Lord see it, and it displease Him, And He turn away His wrath from him."* God will always, in a sense, have a soft spot for people who are hurting or being persecuted.

Your character says a lot about you and is who you are at your core. When something bad happens to someone who was mean to you in the past, does it make you happy? Or does it make you feel bad for what they are going through? David's son Absalom tried to kill him because he wanted total control of the throne. He had watched his father through the years and didn't learn one thing about character. David didn't celebrate the deaths of those who sought to kill him; he was saddened. *God sees the heart of a person, and He wants your heart to be like His.*

When someone dies without knowing God, God is very much saddened *because that person never got to see all that God has for their life and all He has to give to them—His love, His joy, and eternity.* God's character is always exemplary, and although David wasn't perfect, he followed after the Lord. David's character lined up with God's character. *God wants you to have exemplary character, no matter what the situation is in your life. He wants you to continually represent the kingdom of God no matter what, especially when you fall short of His glory.* David is remembered for how he always trusted God even when he committed sin. In the end, David said in 2 Samuel 22:2-4, *"The Lord is my rock and my fortress and my deliverer; The God of my strength, in whom I will trust; My shield and the horn of my salvation, My stronghold and my refuge; My Savior, You save me from violence. I will call upon the Lord, who is worthy to be praised; So, shall I be saved from my enemies."* Living for God, trusting God, and emanating godly character is all that's important in this life. *Then you will see how far He will take you in life. He is who will get you further in life.*

> *Exemplary God, Jehovah Lemofett, I want my character to represent Your character. I will be humble, forgiving, caring, loving, and kind to everyone, especially to my enemies. I will not rejoice when I see people suffering who hurt me, but I will pray for them. I will think about their salvation, just like You think about mine. I thank You, Lord, that I should have a heart after You. In Jesus' name I pray. Amen.*

_____

_____

_____

_____

_____

_____

_____

_____

20

YOUR *GREETING*

Now behold, Boaz came from Bethlehem, and said to the reapers, "The Lord be with you!" And they answered him, "The Lord bless you!"
—*Ruth 2:4*

As Boaz returned from Bethlehem, he greeted his employees with a godly blessing. When was the last time your employer did this? Let's take it a step further: when was the last time a family member or a friend greeted you with a godly blessing? Let's take it still another step further: when was the last time *you* greeted someone with a godly blessing?

People today often greet with a "hello," "what's up?" "how are you doing?"—or with no cordiality at all. How you feel personally is sometimes reflected in how you greet people. The rule of thumb used to be, if you didn't sleep in the same bed with someone that night, you would say good morning to them. But that practice is slowly being phased out. So how about redeeming an old practice and greeting someone with "The Lord be with you!"

This is what God calls you to do each day. *He wants you to put Him first with your words.* As you speak godly words over each other, the atmosphere of your life changes. Imagine greeting someone with, *"The Lord be with you!"* and they reply, *"The Lord bless you!"* How much better would each of your lives be if you're able to go through each day continually reflecting on the positive that God has for you? Imagine hearing those words every moment of your day. Would you have time to think about the things that are being thrown at you by the devil?

This passage in Ruth is a reminder to treat each other with godly respect—just like Boaz did with his employees. Why would Boaz want his workers to have this blessing from God? Because if his workers are blessed, his business is blessed. You can change the world with this simple greeting of godly love. Teach others how to do the same. *People may respond at first with a thank you. But being consistent with this simple greeting may lead them to ask how to respond.*

> *Today, Father, I will start greeting people with a smile. I will bless people with Your blessings. I will speak life into everyone I meet. I will treat people with love today, no matter how they treat me. I will not let this world determine who I am but allow You to determine who I am. I will speak life into people's lives no matter if they like or dislike me, or I them. It's not about me but about You! In Jesus' name I pray. Amen.*

21

YOUR *SELF-CONTROL*

Be sober, be vigilant, because your adversary the devil walks about like a roaring lion, seeking whom he may devour.
—*1 Peter 5:8*

I f you were to go for a hike on an unfamiliar trail, you would probably keep a lookout for things that could cause you harm. If the trail was familiar, you would know where the dangers are and would be able to avoid them. You could focus your attention on things that are different or that you didn't notice before. This is what God is telling you in 1 Peter 5:8—*to be vigilant or alert* when it comes to the devil. The devil will try to set pitfalls, snags, obstacles, wooden roadblocks, or whatever he can to prevent you from getting closer to eternity. The devil is trying to stop you from getting closer to God. Notice the passage doesn't say, "the devil will stop you." Do the police physically stop the car when they are trying to pull it over? Or does the person who is in control of the vehicle pull over and stop? The devil can't stop you, but he can *make you think there's nowhere else to go.*

Within this scripture, God tells you *to be sober or have self-control first.* He knows that certain things in this world will be desirable to you. *This is where your self-control will be needed.* God has already shown you what or who may cause harm to you. *The closer you are to God, the easier it is to see the pitfalls in your life. The closer you are to God, the less desirable things will be that aren't of God.* Does God tempt you? No. Does God stop you from being tempted? No. But He has given you the ability to control yourself. The scripture says, "Be sober," not "Let God sober you." You are not a puppet for the Lord; He wants you to make the choice. Think about Adam and Eve and the tree of knowledge. You are in control and must learn to practice self-control (see 1 Corinthians 10:13).

"Your adversary the devil walks about like a roaring lion, seeking whom he may devour." God will show you what will cause you harm, but are you on the lookout for the harmful things in your life? How do lions hunt for their prey? They stalk them and wait until they are distracted to attack. A gang of meerkats always has someone standing tall as a lookout. That meerkat doesn't allow itself to get distracted because the meerkat knows there is danger out there—danger that wants to devour it and the members of its gang. Being sober and vigilant isn't just for your sake but for the sake of those around you whom you care about. *That's why God said to be sober and vigilant.*

Heavenly Father, I thank You that You have given me the ability to have self-control. I thank You, Lord, that my love for Christ compels me to want to live an uncompromising life. I believe in You and Your Word. I will have self-control. I will be on the alert for the devil's pitfalls. I will walk with confidence, knowing that Christ gave me the strength to turn away from the devil's pitfalls. I will be sober and vigilant. In Jesus' name I pray. Amen.

22

YOUR *TRUST*

16 And the Lord said to him, "Surely I will be with you, and you shall defeat the Midianites as one man." 17 Then he said to Him, "If now I have found favor in Your sight, then show me a sign that it is You who talk with me."
—*Judges 6:16-17*

Trusting the Lord can be hard to do when you are in the middle of a crisis. God says, "I will be with you, and you shall defeat [your enemy]," even if you don't believe in yourself. Here is the most amazing thing: you don't need to put your trust in yourself—you put your trust in God. Stand strong in faith, and say to yourself, *I don't care what things look like. I don't care what I am going through. I don't care what my enemy has said. I only care what God, Yahweh, Jehovah has said to me.*

Gideon, who God told will defeat Israel's enemies, the Midianites, didn't believe Him, nor did he believe he was even speaking with God. So he asked God to show him a sign. Israel had been under constant oppression by the Midianites for seven years. They had been praying and crying out to God throughout those seven years, with no results. *But you must recognize that when you pray,*

God immediately hears and responds. Just because you can't see change yet doesn't mean nothing is happening. God is working behind the scenes and will reveal His will when the time is right. God, in His amazing and incredible holiness, is still humble and not angry with us due to our unbelief. He will strengthen your unbelief. Because of His humility, God showed Gideon the sign he asked for. He told him to put the meat and the unleavened bread on the rock and pour out the broth on top of the food. Then, God used the staff in His hand to bring fire up from the rock to consume the food. After, He immediately "departed out of his sight."

Gideon didn't prepare the food offering until after he encountered God. He had to take time to make the food, and God stayed where He met Gideon until Gideon returned. Even after God proved to Gideon who He was, Gideon still asked for three more signs in order for him to truly trust Him. Through it all, God didn't get angry with Gideon. He could have easily said, "Don't you know who I AM?" In His humility, God is patient with you and will wait until you are ready to receive Him, because He loves you and favors you. *He will show you sign after sign to sustain and increase your faith. When you are ready, you will find out, like Gideon did, that God is right where you met Him. He is waiting on you so He can move you forward. Think about this, your unbelief slows down your change or blessing, because God will not move you forward until He knows you're ready!* After their first encounter, God said to Gideon, "Peace be with you," and Gideon called God "Jehovah Shalom," the Lord of Peace. *Trust God so you can have Peace. God will not rush you nor, especially, His process when He is about to invoke a change in your life.*

Jehovah Shalom, I come to You and believe in what You have said to me. I trust that it is You. I don't want to slow down what You have for me. God, I trust what You have said. I thank You for having patience with me. Lord, I want what You have for me on Your time. I know that when You allow my change or blessing to happen, it will be because You know I am ready to receive it. God, prepare me to receive from You. In Jesus' name I pray. Amen!

_____

_____

_____

_____

_____

_____

_____

_____

_____

_____

_____

23

YOUR *POSSIBILITIES*

"For with God nothing will be impossible."
—Luke 1:37

You may be facing what you feel is an impossible circumstance. You may go to bed each night with something lingering over your life or your family. When you wake up, hoping to feel better, the devil reminds you of your struggle. Do this: stop, take a deep breath, and give God the biggest praise you have ever given Him. *"For with God nothing will be impossible."*

Stop focusing on your problems and exercise your faith in God. It's time to work out your faith. This will take a lot of work, so much so that all you can do at the end of your day is rest. That's the place God has called you to be today. He wants you to trust that He can and will do all things for you. You can rest in Him.

Hebrews 4:5 says, "And again in this place: They shall not enter My rest." How can you trust God when you are not in the right place to enter His rest? Spending time in prayer and praise, studying His Word, and worshiping takes you into God's presence. Once you arrive in the place God has for you, then you can trust He is *Jehovah əv ee efshar*

(אלוהים של הבלתי אפשרי) *(God of the impossible)*. Be like
Mary the mother of Jesus and say to God, "Let it be to me
according to Your word" (Luke 1:38).

*Take a moment and speak the words of Christ over your
situation.* Tell your problem that it will go no further than
this moment—to get out of your way. It is just an obstacle
that's trying to stop you from arriving in God's presence.
The ocean looks extremely wide today, but trust God and
cross the ocean. Once you step into the water, you will see
that it's not an ocean you have to cross but a stream. And
God will hold back the water so you can cross on dry land.
"For with God nothing is impossible."

> *Our Father who art in Heaven, I come to You
> today to say I trust You. God, take me to that
> place You have set aside for me to enter Your
> rest. I have situations in my life that seem to
> me to be impossible to overcome. Right now,
> God, I take my focus off my situation and put
> my focus on You. I know in You, Lord, I have
> victory. My situation will no longer hold me
> captive because You, Jesus, have set me free. I
> thank You, God, for handling every situation
> that will come against me today, tomorrow,
> and each day to come. In Jesus' name I pray.
> Amen.*

24

YOUR *FIGHT*

"Do not be afraid of them. Remember the Lord, great and awesome, and fight for your brethren, your sons, your daughters, your wives and your houses."
—*Nehemiah 4:14b*

There are times in your life when you are going to have to fight. But *how* you fight is the important thing. In this passage, Nehemiah was talking to the Israelites about their enemy who was coming against them as they rebuilt the wall of Jerusalem. He was telling them to stand up and fight for themselves and for each other—to watch each other's backs while they rebuilt the wall. But they needed to be ready to fight a physical battle as well, if need be.

God wants you to stand up and fight "the them." He will lead you through your battles, and He will fight for you. But you need to be prepared with the right weapons. First, when you wake up, you should communicate with your battle Planner through *prayer*. Then, open your battle plan, the *Holy Bible*, and study the Word of God to understand your plan of attack. You should then enter into thanksgiving through *worship*, thanking God for leading you in the battle.

Through it all, God reminds you that you don't have to be afraid of the "them" in your life. Who and what are the "them"? The "them" are fear, worry, disappointments, hardships, struggles, and heartaches. The "them" are people who talk about you, people who want to harm you, people who lie about you, people who try to deceive you, or people who don't like you because of your walk with Christ. The "them" is anything coming against you that's not of God.

Sometimes, in order to deal with the "them," you must utilize a stronger weapon. Jesus said your stronger weapon is *prayer and fasting*. Jesus said, "This kind can come out by nothing but prayer and fasting" (Mark 9:29). When you come up against a strong, stubborn "them," let go of everything and let God take over. When you fast, you are telling God that you give it all to Him. That in faith, you are trusting that *He will handle the "them"* because *He is great and awesome*. Don't be afraid of the "them"; *just remember that the Lord fights for your brethren, your sons, your daughters, your spouse, your household, and you.*

> *Today, Lord, I will go into battle with the right weapons. I will pray to You constantly. I will study Your Word, the Holy Bible, daily. I will worship You always. I will fast in order to strengthen my faith in You. I am not afraid of the "them" because I know You are great and awesome, and You fight for me. In Jesus' name I pray. Amen!*

_____

_____

_____

25

YOUR *POWER*

Finally, my brethren, be strong in the Lord and in the power of His might.
—Ephesians 6:10

I n a fight, you want a strong person to fight with you because you know that no matter what, if the fight turns sideways, you still have a strong teammate by your side. The Philistines thought with Goliath on their side they could defeat anyone or anybody who came against them. But the Philistines didn't expect Goliath, as big as he was, to lose to David, as small as he was. David was a big man spiritually, for He walked with the Lord. You are as big as God's power is in your life.

Goliath thought that because of his strength, his size, his abilities, and his might, he would defeat the Israelites single-handedly. But that's the problem with Goliath—he relied on his own abilities, unlike David who did everything with the Lord's power. David knew that His power in him would be the force to defeat Goliath. David fought this fight with God's strength, size, abilities, and might. And if you don't know, he won.

The question is, *whose strength and might are you fighting your battles with? Are you fighting them standing on your own two feet? Or are you fighting them kneeling and standing on God's two feet?* You are encouraged today to surrender and kneel before the King. Allow Him to rise and fight your battles. Remember, "the battle is not yours, it's the Lord's" (1 Samuel 17:47). Today is the day for you to "Finally, my brethren, *be strong in the Lord* and in the power of His might."

God wants you to rest in Him. For when you rest in Jesus, you are strong in the Lord. For when you rest in God, you are in the power of His might. God will handle everything that's coming against you—all of your issues, situations, problems, and sicknesses, and your sinful nature. *You don't have to endure on your own.*

> *Today, Father, show me how to rely on Your strength and might. I am big not because of who I am but because of who You are. I thank You, Lord, for fighting each and every battle that comes my way. I thank You, Lord, for fighting the battles I can see and the ones I can't see. I thank You, Lord, that You are handling every situation that's current in my life as well as the situations that will arise later in my life. You, Jesus, are my strength and my power. I will do all things through Christ who strengthens me. I stand tall today because You are tall. In Jesus' name I pray. AMEN!*

26

YOUR *HUNGER*

*"I know how to be abased, and I know how to abound.
Everywhere and in all things, I have learned both to be full
and to be hungry, both to abound and to suffer need."*
—*Philippians 4:12*

Have you ever had a wonderful meal at a restaurant and were truly full? Yet you still had room for dessert. That's how you are to be with God. You are to be full of the Word yet still hunger for the Word. You are to be full of the Spirit but still hunger for the Spirit. You are to always have that hunger and passion for God, no matter how long you have known Him.

Paul said that he knew how to live in humility and in prosperity. Why would Paul need to make this statement? Because you need to understand how to be prosperous yet humble. Some believe all prosperous people are arrogant, and still others think to be humble you can't be prosperous. But Paul said you must be both, but not in the way you think! Arrogance is based on selfish pride, so you must be humble in order to show people love. Through the love you give, you will dwell in the prosperity of the Lord. God said, "Do not worry about tomorrow" (Matthew 6:34). *He says that He will supply all your needs,* just like He does for the birds (Matthew 6:25-34).

Finally, Paul said you should remember to be prosperous and still suffer needs. What does this mean? How do you live like you have everything but still acknowledge your needs? When you have Jesus, you have everything—but you still need Jesus every day. When you live with an authentic need for Jesus, you are telling God that you want more of Him. *Live today in the fullness of Christ, and remember your need for Him* every second of the day. *He is your air and your food.*

> *Today, Lord, I am here to say I need You. I hunger for You, even though I know I have all of You. I will not let my desire, my passion, my longing, and my hunger for You go stagnate. I will always want more of You each day. I will stay full of Your Word and will still hunger for Your Word. I will never get enough of You, even when I am in the midst of Your presence. In Jesus' name I pray. Amen.*

27

YOUR *HIM*

15 But Hannah answered and said, "No, my lord, I am a woman of sorrowful spirit. I have drunk neither wine nor intoxicating drink but have poured out my soul before the Lord. 16 Do not consider your maidservant a wicked woman, for out of the abundance of my complaint and grief I have spoken until now."
—1 Samuel 1:15-16

When you pray, do you know you are writing a letter to God? The wonderful thing about writing a letter is that it makes things personal to God. You are writing your words upon God's heart—and He will never cast aside your prayers.

When you write your letters to God, are you writing your letter in pencil or in ink? Before electronic organizers, tablets, and cell phones, you had to write down appointments on paper. Scheduling a meeting or an appointment would involve writing with pencil or ink. If someone penciled you in, it meant the activity was unsure or unconfirmed. If someone scheduled with ink, they likely had no intention of changing their plans with you. Are you writing your letter to God in pencil or in ink?

In 1 Samuel 1, Hannah had been barren for years and felt like God wasn't hearing her prayers. Many of you can relate to this feeling of speaking to the wind. But it wasn't that God didn't hear her prayers; it was that her prayers stemmed from a place of bitterness and sorrow. First Samuel 1:10 says, "And she was in bitterness of soul, and prayed to the Lord and wept in anguish." When Hannah was praying, she was praying from the source of her bitterness. She was praying from her frustration. *Take notice, though, that Hannah never stopped praying!* It wasn't until she prayed from her heart that God answered her prayers: "And it happened, as she continued praying before the Lord, that Eli watched her mouth. Now Hannah spoke in her heart; only her lips moved, but her voice was not heard. Therefore, Eli thought she was drunk" (1 Samuel 1:12-13).

God wants you to lay your burdens on Him, but He doesn't want you to stay in a place of bitterness. *God said He wants you to put your "Heart In Mine": HIM. He wants you to come, from your heart to the Heart of the matter: HIM.* You will have issues and hurts, but only once you get to the *HIM* will your prayers be answered. Once you finally have enough and get tired of soaking in your sorrow, you will be able to *pour out your soul before the Lord.* Hannah said, "for out of the abundance of [her] complaint and grief" she was able to talk to God. Realize that God isn't simply moved by your tears but by your *heart.* It's time to put your complaints and grief aside and put your heart in *HIM. It's time to write your letter to God in ink. It's time to write or speak to God from your heart, not from your hurt. Put your prayers in HIM!*

Dear Lord, I have been disappointed and hurt. I have been bitter because of my disappointments and hurts. I don't care what it looks like. I don't care how it was. I don't care how things went down in my past. I don't care who hurt me or disappointed me. I will not be bitter anymore. I will not be sorrowful anymore. I will rejoice because You are God. I am putting my prayers and my words into Your heart. I am putting everything in HIM. I am putting my pain, my hurt, my disappointments, my failures, my sorrows, my bitterness, my lack, and everything that's stopping me from speaking to You from my heart into Your Heart. I give it all to HIM. I pour out my soul to You and ask You to pour out Your Spirit in me. I will now receive from HIM. From my heart to Yours. In Jesus' name I pray. AMEN!

28

YOUR *PRAISE*

And when he had consulted with the people, he appointed those who should sing to the LORD, and who should praise the beauty of holiness, as they went out before the army and were saying: "Praise the LORD, For His mercy endures forever."
—*2 Chronicles 20:21*

You ought to praise God because His mercy endures forever. People may say, "Why do you sing and shout?" or, "That's why I don't go to church, because of all of that carrying on you people do! Is it really necessary?" Let's think about it. Yes, it is, because God knows all about you and everything you have done, and yet He still gives you mercy. This is the answer to the questions these people ask: You praise God because of His mercy. *He knows the things that you have done, which no one else knows. Again, what no one else knows BUT GOD!*

Psalm 136:1 says, "Oh, give thanks to the LORD, for He is good! For His mercy endures forever." When was the last time you showed someone mercy? The word *mercy* has several meanings, but they are all the same: *mercy*: (1) kind and compassionate treatment; *clemency (mercy, especially toward an offender or enemy: leniency)*; (2) a disposition to be forgiving and kind; (3) alleviation of distress: relief. It doesn't matter the numerous definitions. The point is that God's mercy for you never ends. *He will always give you relief!*

Because His mercy for you never ends, you should always sing and praise Him. Psalm 135:3 says, "Praise the Lord, for the Lord is good; Sing praises to His name, for it is pleasant." *To praise Him is to express admiration to Him. To sing to Him is to use your voice to elevate words of admiration by vocalizing it in a musical tone.* Have you done that today? God wants to hear you sing to Him every day. Don't wait for someone to lead you into praise and worship. *It doesn't matter how you think you sound to others; it only matters how you sound to your merciful God. Sing from your heart, and you will receive God's heart.*

Those who lead you in praise and worship serve a wonderful purpose. This scripture says, "He appointed those who should sing to the LORD, and who should praise the beauty of holiness, *as they went out before* the army." They are to lead you, the army of God, into the spiritual battle against the enemy. These individuals are not perfect, as only God is perfect. But they must be righteous—as you, yourself, ought to be righteous as you sing in solitary praise.

Psalm 144:9a says, *"I will sing a new song to You, O God." When was the last time you sang a new song to God? What is your new song today?*

Almighty God, I lift up my voice to You today to sing a song to You. I will show You admiration with my personal song, singing a new song to You. I know You know all about me, yet You still show me mercy. I will vocalize my admiration to You because Your mercy endures forever; Your mercy endures forever. I thank You, Lord, for Your mercy and grace, and I lift my voice to extol You. In Jesus' name I pray. Amen!

29

YOUR *PLEASING*

With goodwill doing service, as to the Lord, and not to men.
—Ephesians 6:7

I t is plain and simple: you are to please God, not men. When you go about your daily tasks, do you stop and ask yourself, *What does God think about this? Do you ask, Is God pleased with what I am doing?* You are to die to your flesh daily. Putting God as the focus for the reason you do what you do is following God's command to do unto Him, not unto man.

Why shouldn't you try to please people? Because people's feelings or opinions change so easily. God never changes; therefore, you don't have to wonder if what you are doing pleases Him. When you study God's Word each day, you are pleasing Him. When you pray and ask God to guide you each day, you are pleasing Him. When you speak love to someone, you are pleasing Him. When you're seeking after God in all your ways, you are pleasing Him. It's not a mystery how to please God. He shows us how in His Word. *Human feelings waver from moment to moment, but God's feelings never waver. He doesn't operate based on feelings but according to what is just and holy.*

By knowing what God thinks, you are able to please Him and thereby have life more abundantly. In order to know who you are, you must first know who He is. Stop worrying about what family, friends, co-workers, or the world thinks about you. *Place your life into God's hands and jump for joy because of what He thinks about you. Life is "easy" when you are doing everything unto Him. Let me clarify: I didn't say life will not have hard times. I didn't say life will not have tough days. You will have tough days, and you will have rough days. But when those days come, stop and focus on Him. That's when life becomes easy because it isn't you who ultimately handles the issues in life; it is the Father. As Jesus said in Matthew 11:29-30, "Take My yoke upon you and learn from Me, for I am gentle and lowly in heart, and you will find rest for your souls. For My yoke is easy and My burden is light."*

> *Today, Father, I will look to please You. You are my everything. You were with me in the beginning, and You will be with me until the end. I choose to serve You, not the world. I will put You first. My good will service is done for You. Mankind has nothing for me, but You have everything for me. I thank You, and I praise You. In Jesus' name I pray. Amen.*

_____

_____

_____

_____

_____

30

YOUR *NEARNESS*

> [23] *"Am I a God near at hand," says the* LORD, *"And not a God afar off?* [24] *Can anyone hide himself in secret places, so I shall not see him?" says the* LORD; *"Do I not fill heaven and earth?" says the* LORD.*
> —Jeremiah 23:23-24*

There will be days when you feel alone. There will be days when you don't feel like God is there. There will be days when you call on the name of Jesus, and you will not feel Him near. But the truth is, He never leaves your side. He is just waiting to act in His perfect timing. *Shake it off because He is right here!*

When you feel like you are all alone and no one cares for you, God does. Because of the omnipresence of God, He is always, always near! It's like someone in a diving bell being dropped into the ocean—they can't feel the water surrounding them because of the barrier between, but they know the water is there. It's the same way with God. If you don't feel God near, it's because you have put up a barrier between you and Him. You must tear down this barrier to feel the Lord's presence more closely. *Tear down your barrier today!*

God is everywhere; therefore, you can't hide anything from Him. You may hear stories of salvation where the individual says, "When God found me." But God doesn't have to *find* you; He already knows where you are and what you are going through. He said, *"Am I a God near at hand?"* When Saul had his conversion to Paul, Jesus stopped him on the road—He did not need to seek him out. When God walked through the garden of Eden, He asked Adam, *"Where are you?" God knew where Adam was, but Adam didn't understand where he was in his mind, his spirit, or his walk with God.* Adam was lost even though his eyes were open. Are you lost today? *Just open your eyes to God, and you will see His vast glory.*

When you come into God's presence, you do not *find* God. Rather, your eyes are open to God, and you can see Him more clearly. *His glory is so vast, nothing can contain the glory of God.*

> *Glorious God, I am glad today that my eyes are open to You. I know that Your glory fills me up. If I feel You aren't near me, I know You are still right there, surrounding me with Your glory. You are always right here with me, and no matter what I am going through, I will fear not. Since You always surround me, I know I am covered by You today and every day. I thank You for Your covering. In Jesus' name I pray. Amen.*

31

YOUR *CARES*

⁶ Therefore humble yourselves under the mighty hand of God,
that He may exalt you in due time, ⁷ casting all your care upon
Him, for He cares for you.
—*1 Peter 5:6-7*

There are five words that stand out in this passage: *humble, mighty, exalt, casting,* and *care*. God has first asked you to show meekness. Then He reminds you that He has great, immeasurable power. He tells you because of your modesty, He will raise you up out of the darkness. Furthermore, He tells you to throw the things that weigh heavy on you onto Him—your worries, troubles, distresses, and grief. He does this because *He loves you.*

Pause and take a look at this part of the scripture: "casting all your care upon Him, for He cares for you." *Isn't it amazing how you change just one little thing, and it becomes something else?* The word *care* means to worry or distress, but it also means to be attentive to detail. How you use the word in a sentence changes its meaning. God doesn't only change the meaning of *care* for you, but He makes it continuous by adding an "s." He will never stop caring *for you.*

God understands that humility is not easy. But He shows you that if you can recognize *how great He is* and show Him *the reverence He deserves, He will raise you up.* God goes even further than that: He will praise you. In the story of Job, God told the devil to do what He wanted to him, apart from killing him. That no matter what Satan did, Job would not curse Him. God praised Job before Satan.

Let this scripture sink into your soul today. It shows you who God is, how He wants you to carry yourself, how He feels about you, what He wants you to do, and what He will do for you.

No matter what today looks or feels like, remember these words: "in due time." God will raise you up at the right time. Store this scripture in your heart because your time is coming. *Keep praising Him, keep exalting Him, and keep casting your cares upon Him, for your time is coming. Then you will see that your time is now.*

> *Mighty and magnificent God, I come before You with humility. I exalt Your mighty name. I bow down, throwing all of my worries upon You. I know You can handle it because You are God alone, and there is none like You. I thank You that my due time is now. I thank You that You told me today that I am due, and I receive what You have set aside for me today and each day to come. In the name of Jesus, I pray. AMEN!*

32

YOUR *PLEASANTNESS*

²⁰But she said to them, "Do not call me Naomi; call me Mara, for the Almighty has dealt very bitterly with me. ²¹I went out full, and the Lord has brought me home again empty. Why do you call me Naomi, since the Lord has testified against me, and the Almighty has afflicted me?"
—*Ruth 1:20-21*

God will have you return back to the place where He wants to bless you. Just like Naomi, many people get mad at God when they feel He has afflicted them with hardship. Let's clear this up: God doesn't want you to live a life of hardship, and He will not bring hardship upon you. Rather, God will use your hardship to bless you. After Naomi's husband and sons died, she felt like God had left her. In her eyes, just like how you may feel when hardship comes, she felt that God caused these things to happen to her. Yes, Naomi's family died. Yes, Naomi felt like she lost everything. But Naomi, in her bitter state, didn't see what God was doing for her. She couldn't see what God was doing in her personal life as well as through her daughter-in-law, Ruth, who wouldn't leave her side.

The name *Mara* means bitter, and the name *Naomi* means pleasant. The devil wants you to feel like a *Mara*. He wants you to feel disappointed in God, and he wants you to give up on Him. But look at what God did for Naomi. After her husband and sons died, Ruth stayed with her. *Naomi didn't have to grieve alone.* Naomi and Ruth had to travel over sixty miles to get back to Bethlehem. *God protected them as they traveled,* and they were able to make it back to Naomi's hometown safely. When they arrived, Naomi was greeted by her people with open arms—*she had favor amongst them.* Even though they lost everything, *God provided a place for Naomi and Ruth to live.* When you live in a bitter place like *Mara,* you can't see what God has done for you and where He is taking you.

So why did Naomi and Ruth have to return to Bethlehem? So God could bless them. From their tragedy came glory. Ruth went to work in a field, and not just any field but the field of a close relative named Boaz. *This wasn't a coincidence.* Who had a hand in all of that? *God!* Through that meeting, Ruth married Boaz, and they had a son named Obed. Obed had a son named Jesse, who had a son named David. When you think God has forgotten you or that He has turned His back on you, you dwell in the bitterness of Mara. It is easy to see God when *He is providing for you; it's hard to see God when you feel you have nothing. God never stop being Jehovah Jireh. He doesn't change; you just stop trusting Him and go to a bitter place.* You may not see what He is doing in your life, but *you must trust that through your hardship He will bless you. God will provide more for you than what you lost. It's time to go back home where you can find your pleasant place of peace in God.*

Jehovah Jireh, I know You are my provider. I will not be bitter when tragedy or hardship hits me. I will rejoice, knowing that You provided for me before and You continue to provide for me now. I may not see what You are doing, God, but I know You are moving on my behalf. I ask You to open my eyes to see what You are doing and where You are taking me. I will believe and trust Your process. I love You, Lord, and I lift my hands to worship You and say thank You! In Jesus' name I pray. Amen!

33

YOUR *STILLNESS*

¹³ And Moses said to the people, "Do not be afraid. Stand still, and see the salvation of the Lord, which He will accomplish for you today. For the Egyptians whom you see today, you shall see again no more forever. ¹⁴ The Lord will fight for you, and you shall hold your peace."
—Exodus 14:13-14

The first part of this scripture tells you, "Do not be afraid." Then it says to "stand still." You live in a world of hustle and bustle—in a world where people are constantly moving from one thing to the next. With the prevalence of social media, the average attention span is said to be three seconds. But God instructed you to learn to *"stand still."* The third thing this scripture tells you is to *"see the salvation of the Lord."* Finally, it says, "He will accomplish for you today."

Don't let anything you are going through cause you to be afraid. Instead, take the time to really "stand still" and listen for the Lord. Once you stop running around trying to solve your own problems, you will be able to "see the salvation of the Lord." For God has told you that *He will accomplish what you have been praying for. You need only to get rid of the distractions that prevent you from seeing what He wants to do for you.*

The reason Moses told the people to "not be afraid" is because even after all the things they had seen God do, they still didn't trust Him. They needed to first trust God—and you do too. Let go of all that you have been told about your situations in life. *"Do not be afraid" of what is coming against you. Then, "stand still" and trust that God will handle everything for you.* When you trust God, you will be able to see what He is doing for you. Why did Moses end with, "He will accomplish for you today"? If you are trying to make everything in your life happen with your own strength instead of letting God show you how to make it happen, you will not allow His full power and blessing into your life. *You must "stand still" so you can hear from Him.* Take the time to "stand still" and let God accomplish what He wants to accomplish in your life today. *Then you will learn that "the Lord will fight for you, and you shall hold your peace."*

You can only pay attention when you're not distracted. Again, I say, you can only pay attention when you aren't distracted!

Heavenly Father, I want to learn more about You today. I want to see Your salvation in my life. So I will stop running around and take the time to stand still. I ask, today, for Your will to be done in my life. I ask You to accomplish the things in my life that I am not able to accomplish. I thank You for fighting my battles and reminding me that the battle isn't mine but the Lord's. In Jesus' name I pray. Amen.

34

YOUR *ASK*

Ask the LORD for rain In the time of the latter rain. The LORD will make flashing clouds; He will give them showers of rain, Grass in the field for everyone.
—Zechariah 10:1

W hen you ask God for something, He will give you more than what you ask for. This scripture starts off with "Ask." You must first open your mouth and "Ask" God for what you need. Then pray for God to move in your life and have patience because He will do it "In the time." Do not try to rush God's timing; He hears what you say and will do what needs to be done. So have faith that what you've asked for is already completed.

The *meat* of this scripture is, after you've asked God to move in your life, He will do more than what you've asked of Him. You ask for a little rain, and "He will give [you] showers of rain." Up until 2016, California was experiencing a terrible drought, so residents kept asking for the relief of rain. Well, eventually in 2017 they got more than what they asked for because it rained so much that parts of California flooded. *That's how it is with God.* When you ask, *He will pour down an overwhelming amount of blessings upon you.* Think about when the Israelites were in the wilderness and asked for food. God said, "I have heard the complaints of the children of Israel. Speak to them, saying, 'At twilight you shall eat meat, and in the morning, you shall be filled with bread. And you shall know that I am the Lord your God.'" *God will provide you with more than you ask, and you will know that He is the Lord.*

Think about this: *"The Lord will make flashing clouds."* God will show you that He is coming to provide for you. He will show you He is coming to answer your prayers. So you must look, wait, and expect God to show up in the situations in your lives. Remember this: in whatever you ask of Him, *He is capable of giving you more than enough.* When people asked Jesus to heal them, *He made them whole.* God will always make you whole. Finally, the downpour is not just for you but to bless those whom God put in your path. There will be "grass in the field for everyone," so ask for your rain to fall, and wait for *your rainstorm*.

> *Today, Lord, I thank You that You will not only send the rain my way but that You are sending the rainstorm. That my storehouse will not have enough room to store what You are sending my way. I glorify in Your presence because what You do for me on earth is great and immeasurable. But what is waiting for me in heaven is glorious. Thank You, Father, that I will have patience to wait on what You are doing. Because what You are doing in my life is so much more than what I see. In Jesus' name I pray. Amen.*

35

YOUR *FORGIVENESS*

And be kind to one another, tenderhearted, forgiving one another, even as God in Christ forgave you.
—Ephesians 4:32

Forgiveness is a tough thing to do at times. People will cause you pain, hurt, or broken heartedness. You may tell yourself, *I don't want to ever see them again.* But can you live a blessed life with unforgiveness in your heart?

Why should you forgive? When you have forgiveness in your heart, you have love in your heart. Since God has unending forgiveness for you, He asks the same *from* you. Matthew 18:21-22 says, "Then Peter came to Him and said, 'Lord how often shall my brother sin against me, and I forgive him? Up to seven times?' Jesus said to him, 'I do not say to you, up to seven times, but up to seventy times seven.'" Jesus told Peter not to keep score but to always forgive one another.

Forgiveness allows you to live a peaceful life. *Where there is peace there is forgiveness.* Allowing you to be able to have more joy than ever before. Having unforgiveness in your life is hiding bitterness in your heart. You may think forgiving someone means releasing that person from their wrongdoing. That you are forgiving them in order for them to feel better about themselves. Your forgiveness may result in this, but forgiveness is really about *you*. Forgiveness is a give and take. God forgives you so that you, in turn, will walk in Love. God asks you to forgive so you can show His love to others. *In the big picture, forgiveness is all about you being free from sin, pain, heartache, and malice so that you can dwell in Love.*

In the Lord's prayer, Jesus said, "And forgive us our sins, for we also forgive everyone who is indebted to us" (Luke 11:4). Jesus said to *forgive everyone at all times*. You are not to pick and choose who to forgive or what you can forgive people for. Forgive at all times and for all things. *Matthew 6:15 says, "But if ye forgive not men their trespasses, neither will your Father forgive your trespasses."* Let go of all of your past hurts. Call on someone today whom you haven't forgiven so that you can release yourself from the past. *God is your forgiving Father (your FF); why don't you be His forgiving person (His FP)? Forgiveness may seem tough to do at times, but you can do it!*

> *My forgiving Father, I thank You for forgiving me. I ask You to show me how to forgive others. Let me not have malice or bitterness in my heart. In spite of all the things I have done, You have forgiven me. I will live and treat people the way You treat me. I will forgive because it's the way to Your heart. I ask You to soften my heart in order for me to have true forgiveness. When I forgive someone, I will be like You, Father, and never mention it to that person again. I will truly forgive and forget so I may surround myself with Love. In Jesus' name I pray. Amen!*

36

YOUR *STRIFELESS*

For men verily swear by the greater: and an oath for
confirmation is to them an end of all strife.
—Hebrews 6:16 (KJV)

*D*o *you need strife?* Strife will disrupt your life. It may
even cause people to get sick. So how do you get rid
of it? In a dispute or an argument, people sometimes say, "I
swear on my mother." They might even go as far as saying,
"I swear on my mother's grave." The courts ask people to
swear on the Holy Bible. Or people may just say, "I swear I
am telling the truth." When someone swears on something
greater than them, their strife may come to an end. But
remember what God said: "Let your 'Yes' be 'Yes,' and your
'No,' 'No'" (Matthew 5:37).

Strife comes to an end when you confirm things will be
settled—when you know that whatever the issue is, it will
be handled. You can then let go of the strife in your life. To
prove to mankind that He would take care of them, God
made an oath, swearing on Himself. Hebrews 6:13 says,
"For when God made a promise to Abraham, because He
could swear by no one greater, He swore by Himself." *He*
did this to say that He will always take care of you. He did this

to tell you that all your strife will come to an end. He did this to tell you that there is no one greater than Him.

Some people think they aren't living if they don't have strife in their life. God doesn't want you to have strife in your life. But when you do, He wants you to look to Someone greater than you to resolve it. God has been here from the beginning. He is the Alpha and Omega, the beginning and the end. *God is the end of all strife.* He wants you to know it's time to let all strife go. In order to do this, *your oath of confirmation is Jesus.*

> *My omnipotent God, You are astonishing, for You are the end of all strife. I will no longer welcome strife in my life. I will welcome Your Salem, Your Shalom. I will have peace in my life. I know Jesus is my oath of confirmation to end the strife in my life. Thank You, Jesus. In Jesus' name I pray. Amen.*

37

YOUR *DOUBTLESS*

*But let him ask in faith, with no doubting, for he who doubts
is like a wave of the sea driven and tossed by the wind.*
—James 1:6

D oubt kills dreams. Doubt causes confusion. Doubt
prolongs blessings from happening. Doubt will
cause you to miss what God has already set aside for you.
You're probably thinking, *If God has already set it aside for
me, why would doubt cause me not to receive it?* Your doubt
tells God that you're not ready. God will supply all your
needs, but you must be in a place to receive all that He has
for you. When it comes to provisions, you will not lack.
But when you doubt, you will lack life in the fullness of
God.

Why do people doubt? Because of what looks like failure
in their lives or other people's lives, they find cause to
doubt. But just because something didn't work before
doesn't mean it will not work this time. *When you line
up with God*, it will work on time. Thomas Edison was
fired from his first two jobs for being "non-productive."
As an inventor, Edison made one thousand unsuccessful
attempts at inventing the light bulb. When a reporter
asked, "How did it feel to fail one thousand times?"

Edison replied, "I didn't fail one thousand times. The light bulb was an invention with one thousand steps." God wants you to remove all doubt from your prayers *because sometimes there are steps your prayers must go through before they are answered.*

You must have patience to wait on the Lord. You must have faith, knowing God heard your prayers and will answer them. You must not be double-minded. James 1:7-8 says, "For let not that man suppose that he will receive anything from the Lord; he is a double-minded man, unstable in all his ways." The word *suppose* means to assume to be real or true for the sake of an argument or explanation. In other words, you don't really believe it will happen. God said that is being double-minded. God doesn't want you to suppose, but He expects you to have unwavering faith in Him. Mark 11:23 says, "For assuredly, I say to you, whoever says to the mountain, 'Be removed and be cast into the sea,' and does not doubt in his heart, but believes that those things he says will be done, he will have whatever he says." This was spoken after Jesus told the fig tree, "Let no one eat fruit from you ever again." Mark 11:20 says, "Now in the morning, as they passed by, they saw the fig tree dried up from the roots." Each day you wake up is a day closer to you seeing your prayers being answered. *Answered prayers are a day away! It's time to release the doubt and grab hold of your faith. Better yet, grab hold of your doubtless.*

Oh, Heavenly Father, I thank You for removing all doubt from my prayers and my life. I will not be double-minded. I will stand firm on my beliefs. I know that all my prayers, according to Your will, have and will be answered. I will not have doubts about prayers that have yet to be answered. For I know that all my prayers will be answered in due time, according to Your will. It may not be tomorrow or even the next day. But I know each day You breathe life into me is a day closer to my prayers being answered. I trust in You, in the name of Jesus and in the Holy Spirit. In Jesus' name I pray. AMEN!

38

YOUR *LET*

⁴ "But when the kindness and the love of God our Savior toward man appeared, ⁵ not by works of righteousness which we have done, but according to His mercy He saved us, through the washing of regeneration and renewing of the Holy Spirit, ⁶ whom He poured out on us abundantly through Jesus Christ our Savior."
—Titus 3:4-6

When Jesus died on the cross, resurrected from the grave, and ascended to the Father, God poured out the Holy Spirit on you (John 16:5-22). *But you must be willing to receive the Holy Spirit. There are people who are in the midst of the raining down of the Holy Spirit and are wearing a wetsuit and raincoat while holding an umbrella.* The umbrella is your disbelief or lack of faith. The raincoat is the wall you put up to protect yourself from hurt, pain, and disappointment. The wetsuit is the layers of past issues, problems, and attacks that have happened in your life over the years. How can God wash you with the Holy Spirit if you are covered by your past mistakes or choices? You are putting up a barrier from what God has for you. *It's time to let go!*

Scripture says, "not by works of righteousness which we have done, but according to His mercy He saved us." Yes, you work toward righteousness because you want to live a righteous life. You can't save yourself, but you can allow Him to save you. The word *allow* is used because it is your choice. You can choose to live in hell on earth or you can choose, "thy will be done, on earth as it is in heaven." Because of the gift of Jesus, you are made righteous. *It's time to let go!*

The constant pouring of the Holy Spirit is so God can remove that umbrella out of your hands, so God can take that raincoat off of you, and so God can take you out of that wetsuit. The conundrum is that people are holding tightly to their umbrella, raincoat, and wetsuit instead of letting God have it all. It's not complicated! God said, "Come unto me, all ye that labour and are heavy laden, and I will give you rest." The New International Version translated it, *"Come to Me*, all you who are weary and burdened, and I will give you rest." *If you are still holding on to your umbrella, raincoat, and wetsuit, you can't be washed.* Try standing in the rain or taking a shower with all of that on. You will stay dry—the same. *Stop holding on to it and let it go. It's time to let God take it all off and let the Holy Spirit wash you. It is your let, so let it go!*

> *God, pour out Your Holy Spirit on me. Holy Spirit, I ask You to wash me clean. I am letting all of the past, hurts, issues, problems, and hell in my life go. I am here, God, to receive through the washing of regeneration and renewing of the Holy Spirit, whom You poured out on me abundantly through Jesus Christ my Savior. In Jesus' name I pray. Amen.*

39

YOUR *SALVATION*

"Behold, God is my salvation, I will trust and not be afraid;
'For Yah, the Lord, is my strength and song; He also has become
my salvation.'"
—Isaiah 12:2

S alvation: Preservation or deliverance from danger, evil, or difficulty. You could read this scripture and just stop here: "God is my salvation; I will trust and not be afraid." But it goes on to say He is your strength and song! *God is your deliverer. He is your power. He is your vocalized expression.*

Do you trust God? Or are you afraid?

God used the word *behold* here. He did this because He wants you to stop and look at who He is to you. He wants you to see that you can trust Him. He wants you to know where you draw your strength from. *God wants you to know He will protect you from all danger and all evil.* So what do you have to do? All you have to do is trust Him in spite of the problems, the issues, the circumstances, or how things may look. Hold fast to this scripture when things get tough.

Why did God say salvation twice in this passage? He wants you to know that no one else can deliver you. Once you understand there is only one Deliverer, your life will change.

What are you afraid of? *Knowing that your salvation is in God allows you to understand that you are not to be afraid of anything.* It doesn't matter what's coming your way. *Don't be afraid!* It doesn't matter who is coming against you. *Don't be afraid!* It doesn't matter how the situation appears. *Don't be afraid!* God did not give you the spirit of fear. *DO NOT FEAR!* You are strong *because "greater is He that is in you than he that is in the world"* (1 John 4:4 KJV). *Your salvation is in Jesus!*

> *Yahweh, You are my strength and my song. You are my salvation. I will trust You. My deliverance is in Jesus. I thank You for being my Deliverer. Since nothing is greater than You, Lord, nothing can stop what You have for me. It doesn't matter what's coming against me, I will not be afraid anymore. I thank You for my salvation. In Jesus' name I pray. Amen!*

_____

_____

_____

_____

_____

_____

_____

40

YOUR *I AM*

Now I say this, that each of you says, "I am of Paul," or "I am of Apollos," or "I am of Cephas," or "I am of Christ."
—*1 Corinthians 1:12*

Days may be tough sometimes, but you need to remember this scripture. Tell yourself that *"I am of Christ."* You belong to Christ! So tell others you are with Christ. Tell the world that you possess Christ.

Let that boldness rise up in you today to speak those words: *"I am of."* As you do, you ignite something inside you that wants to burst out. Think of a diehard fan of a specific sports team. Do they just say, "I like the team!" No. Usually they make a bold statement and say, "I am a Laker" or "I am a Raider."

To use the words *I am* is to say that you are a part of something. Paul wanted all who call on the name of Jesus to remember that it wasn't just a man who died for them—it was God. They weren't baptized in the name of Paul, Apollos, or Cephas. They were *baptized in the name of Christ*, reminding them that only Christ can save them.

Your *"I AM"* defines who you are, who you are with, and who you will be. Your *"I AM"* starts and ends with Jesus.

What is your "I AM" statement today?

> *Heavenly Father, I come boldly before You and say, "I am of Christ! I am strong in Christ! I am a Christian. I am wonderfully made. I am filled with godly wisdom. I am blessed. I am humble. I am highly favored by God. I am who You say I am! Because I have I AM in me, I have discovered the I AM in me. In Jesus' name I pray. Amen.*

AUTHOR'S AFTERWORD

Now that you have gotten through your forty-day walk with Jesus, let me share why I was led to write these devotionals. I know this information is normally at the beginning of a book, but I wanted you to focus on God, Jesus, and the Holy Spirit—not me. *It's not about me. It's just about Jesus!*

Well, I need to take you back to 2013. At this time, I was already on a deep walk with Christ, but what would happen on February 15th, 2013, would hit me like a brick. Any and everything that transpired after that just kept loading bricks on me. In 1998 I transitioned from being an active Marine to an inactive Marine. Once a Marine, always a Marine. So I started on my next journey in life. I dove into the world of acting—but not really. I became an extra and a stand-in for films, TV, and commercials, but through the blessing of God, I was in SAG (the actor's union) in less than two weeks, which is really hard to do. I guess by now you are wondering, *What does this have to do with February 15th, 2013?* I am getting to that.

In 2010, after being in the acting business for twelve years, and after doing a few films and TV shows here and there, I decided to stop tap dancing and get an agent. Again, God's hands were all over this. Even though it seemed like it took a while, I got my first commercial agent and then a theatrical agent named Eurydice Davis. *Remember that name.* Now you have the backstory of my career as an actor and as a writer, producer, and future director.

Let's get back to February 15th, 2013, the day after Valentine's Day. I would normally call my mom on Valentine's and wish her a happy Valentine's Day. But that day I was busy running around, trying to get all the paperwork done to purchase a new house. Needless to say, I didn't talk to her before she went to work. So I decided I would call her the next day. The next morning I got up, and my wife went to work, my two younger sons went to school, and my oldest was getting ready for work. A friend of mine asked me to write him a scene for his reel. I told him I would write a short story instead. So I sat at the computer to write the script. My plan was to write for a while, then call my mom before noon West Coast time.

As I began writing, my cell phone rang. It was my Aunt Druscilla. I didn't answer it because I knew we would be on the phone for a long time (my family likes to talk). But she called back, so I answered. She told me she was coming by because she was on her way from Murrieta to get some fabric. I found it odd but didn't put too much thought into it. Then my Uncle Ron, her husband, called me. For both of them to call me—that was weird. He told me there was something happening in South Carolina, and I should call home and see what is going on. I hung up and resumed my writing, but I soon decided to make the call to my mother.

I dialed my mother's number, and one of my aunts answered her phone. I asked what was going on. My aunt said, "Audrey is dead." I immediately went into Marine mode. I asked questions about what had happened, and I told her I would fly out the next day.

When I got off the phone, I went right back to writing and didn't know how deeply this news had cut me. Not only had I just heard that my mother, whom I have loved with all my heart, was gone, but the news was given to me like it was an afterthought. I started crying uncontrollably to the point where my oldest son came downstairs and asked me if I was OK. I couldn't speak, so he called my wife and said something was wrong with Daddy. By the time my wife got home, Aunt Druscilla and Cousin Krystina were at the house.

This was the start of my road to depression. The following year in May of 2014, my family and I moved from Montclair to Rancho Cucamonga. On Wednesday of the week of the move, my family and I visited my cousin Crystal, who lived in Burbank. On Friday we were set to move into our new place—the house provided through God's divine providence. As we were finishing up moving everything the day of the move, my cousin Baggy called me and told me that he hadn't heard from Crystal, his daughter, since Wednesday, and he asked me to check on her. I said I would when we got done unloading the moving truck, which ended up taking until 11 p.m. I was still going to go check on Crystal, but I ultimately felt it wasn't safe as tired as I was at the time. I decided to go the next morning after dropping off the moving truck, which was on the way to Burbank.

The next morning, I received a phone call from my cousin's best friend, and she told me that Crystal was rushed to the hospital. When I got there, hospital staff were working on her. The strangest thing: I walked right into the room where they were working on her, and no one stopped me. I looked at her, and she looked at me and said, "Hey, cous, what you doin'?" I said, "I am here to see you and let you know it is going to be all right." She smiled and turned her head back, and that was the last conversation we had.

Even though I was at the hospital every day for two weeks before they decided to let her transition, I felt like I didn't fight hard enough for her. What had happened was that from Wednesday to Saturday, she was on her floor because her blood sugar dropped too low, and she wasn't able to take her insulin. As she took her final breaths, my heart broke. I always saw her as my little sister, even though she was older than me by seven months. I remember her mouthing to me and reaching as she passed away. I hated life and everyone who stood around and didn't fight for her. This event caused me to go further down the road of depression.

Fast-forward to April 2015. Recall that name I told you to remember? Now Eurydice (Eury) Davis comes into play (my theatrical agent). I was on a TV show, and soon after my mother passed away. Eury reached out to me to see if I needed anything or wanted to talk and to tell me she was there for me. I never took her up on that offer because I always saw myself as the helper, not the one that needed help. Well, I wish I had taken her up on that offer because things may have turned out differently.

As deep of a depression that I was in, I remember calling her in March 2015 to tell her if *she* ever needed to talk, I am here for her. I realized later that was the Holy Spirit. See, when you have a relationship with Christ, no matter what the devil throws at you, the foundation is still there.

On April 18th, 2015, I was doing a play, and the actress opposite of me was admiring my progress in the business. She asked me how I get so much work and who my agent was. I told her Eury Davis, and her demeanor changed. I asked what was going on. She said, "The Eury Davis that Twinkie Bryd tweeted about?" She paused and said, "She committed suicide, Darius." Shocked, I said, "Stop playing." She showed me the tweet, and I again went into Marine mode and started to try to contact her. But I soon realized the news was true. This was the last ton of bricks that could have done me in. By this point, Eury had been my agent for over four years. To find out she died, and by suicide for that matter, really pierced my heart because she had always pushed me to succeed, and I saw her as a dear friend. I remembered the last conversation I had with her, and I started crying because this was now three deaths in three years.

I don't know if my family knew how depressed I was back then. I was just going through the motions for a little over three years. I still dabbled in the Word. I went to church. I still prayed but not as frequently. I still taught in children's church, which really maintained in me a desire to stay somewhat present.

Around October 2016, I slowly started to snap out of it by getting into the Word more. I started worshipping more. I started praying more. I started reading a devotional book with the one hundred names of God. Then in January 2017, our church had a corporate fast. I fasted and started reading one of Pastor Diego's devotional books. On the last day, March 4th, 2017, I read the final devotional in his book. When I went to bed that night, my prayer was pure in heart. I simply said, "Father, I would love to write a devotional." Isn't it amazing that you can keep it simple with God? The next morning, March 5th, 2017, I woke up around 4 a.m. Unbeknownst to me, the Lord was waking me up to *write*. I went into prayer and worship, and the next thing I knew, I was on the computer after reading Zephaniah 3:9: "For then I will restore to the peoples a pure language. That they all may call on the name of the Lord. To serve Him with one accord." This became my first devotional.

For the next eighty-one days, I woke up around 4 a.m. with no alarm. No matter how late I went to bed, I would wake up and connect with the Holy Spirit and let what He wanted to be said flow out onto the computer screen. It wasn't until I finished writing each excerpt that I was drawn closer to the peace I was seeking.

This book came out of struggles, brokenness, hardship, depression, and thoughts of suicide, as well as from the hope of knowing that one day all of it will be no more. I always tell my wife in hard times, "And this too shall pass." But I had to get to the place where I said a simple prayer, asking God to use me—and oh, He definitely did. Who knows, one day the Holy Spirit might say it's time to release another forty days of outpouring.

What I know today is that if you are dealing with any challenges or trials right now, there is a tomorrow if the Lord allows. Don't let all that the devil is coming against you with dictate how you live. Let the breath of God the *Pneuma* dictate how you live. I had to realize that I needed to get back to the Foundation who formed all of creation.

If you haven't already accepted Christ in your heart, there is no better time than now. The Lord is knocking, and I pray the journey in this book has brought you to the point where you answer the door. If you, before or while going on your journey in this book, already accepted Jesus as your Lord and Savior, I pray that this book took you to that deeper relationship with Him and that you truly discovered who *I Am* is!

SCRIPTURE INDEX